BiteSize Guitar

A concise, comprehensive guitar method for the complete beginner

Michael Haworth

Acknowledgements

For Kiran, Mo, Jyoti, Priya and Sunny.
Thank you for all your encouragement and support.
I wouldn't have been able to do this without your input.

A big thank you to all the pupils whose comments
and road testing helped me to put the book together.

Special thanks to Stuart and Jenny at TH Media for all their help getting the book published.

ISBN 978-0-9928398-8-8

All compositions, illustrations, music setting, layout and book design by Michael Haworth.

Published by TH Media in Derbyshire in 2019.

Contents

important information

Backing tracks for the pieces in BiteSize Guitar have been written as an aid to learning. Each piece either has an introduction or a count in, and it is recommended that pupils listen to the tracks whilst reading the music to familiarise themselves with the pieces before attempting to play them. Backing tracks for all the pieces are available by visiting **www.michaelhaworth.co.uk** or by scanning the QR code and following the link on the website to **BiteSize Guitar**.

Getting Started

Track 1

Tuning Your instrument

Tuning a guitar can be very daunting at first so it may be an idea to get your guitar teacher to help you. Alternatively, if you don't have a guitar teacher, you can always use a guitar tuner. Guitar tuners come in all sorts of shapes and sizes and are also available as apps. There are plenty to choose from so it's probably best to read reviews or ask for advice from someone you know who plays the guitar. It shouldn't take too long before you get the hang of using one.

Your Guitar

The anatomy of electric and acoustic guitars is similar in many respects and both types of instrument are played in very much the same way.

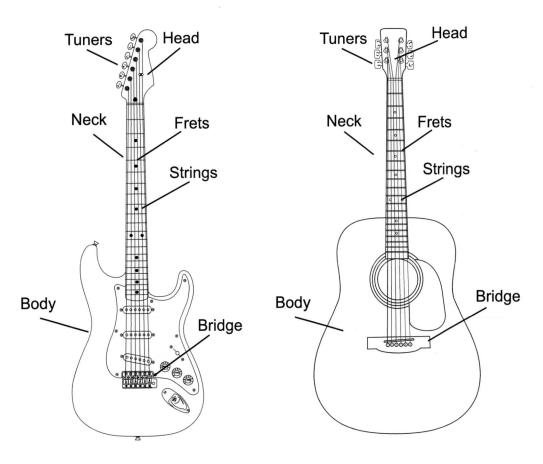

Holding Your Instrument

It is important to hold your instrument correctly to promote good playing habits. Put the body of your guitar on your right leg with the neck of the guitar pointing outwards to your left-hand side. If you are learning as a left-handed player, you will need to do this the opposite way around.

Hold your plectrum (or pick) between your thumb and the outside of your index finger.

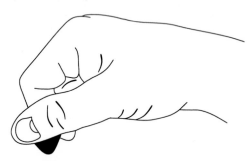

Rest the side of the palm of your hand against the **bridge** of your guitar and pluck the thinnest string with the point of your plectrum. Make sure you are plucking downwards towards the floor. The string you are playing is called **E** or the **first string**.

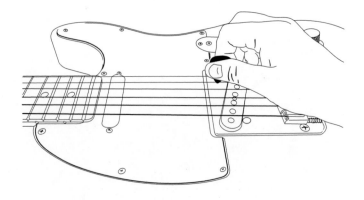

The Pulse

When you listen to a song, you might find yourself tapping your foot or nodding your head in time with the music. When you do this, you are feeling **the pulse**. The pulse is the heartbeat of the music that we listen to. This piece uses our E string. When you see the letter E, play your E string. Rests are silences in music.

Tracks 2 & 3

Pulsar

Start ..../..../....
End ..../..../....

E E E E Rest Rest Rest Rest
(play four times)

Tracks 4 & 5

Blue Surfer

Start ..../..../....
End ..../..../....

This next piece introduces our second string. This string is called **B**. We play our B string in exactly the same way as our E string. Remember to rest your picking hand against your bridge.

E E E E Rest Rest Rest Rest x4

B B B B Rest Rest Rest Rest

E E E E Rest Rest Rest Rest

(repeat piece from the beginning)

Top Tip

Rests in music are as important as the notes. When the music indicates that rests are to be played, you can put your plectrum back on your string to stop it from vibrating. As well as making sure there is silence during the rest, your plectrum will be ready for the next note. If the music you are playing requires you to move onto a different string, you can use part of your picking hand finger or thumb to do this.

Bars

In the following piece, we are going to divide the music into **bars** (or measures). They are separated using **bar lines** (or measure lines). This makes the music easier to read. In each of the bars, there are four beats of the pulse. The bar lines are a visual aid to help us read the music, but they don't affect the sound or how we play the notes.

Tracks 6 & 7

Who is it?

Start ..../..../....

End ..../..../....

Listen out for the introduction played on synthesizer and piano. The guitar begins after the drum fill. Make sure you play the first two lines twice.

E E Rest Rest | B B Rest Rest |
⎫
⎬ x2
E E Rest Rest | B Rest Rest Rest |
⎭

E E Rest Rest | x4

E E Rest Rest | B B Rest Rest |

E E Rest Rest | E (let note ring) ‖

A double bar line tells us that it's the end of the piece of music.

Summary

In this lesson we have learnt how to:

- Hold our guitar and plectrum correctly.
- Identify the pulse.
- Play our E and B strings.
- Play three pieces of music using notes. and rests.
- Divide music up into bars using bar lines.

Things To Remember

- Good posture promotes good playing habits.
- Rest your picking hand on the bridge of your guitar.
- Pick the string downwards towards to floor.
- Rests are silences in music.

Rhythm

In its simplest form, we can look at rhythm as being patterns of long and short sounds and silences. Already we have used notes (sounds) and rests (silences) in our pieces that we have learnt from Lesson 1. In this lesson, we are going to begin to look at how we notate (write down) these sounds.

The Crotchet

 This is a note. It is called a **crotchet** (or quarter note) and it tells us to play a sound. It is worth **one beat** of the pulse and can be written with its **stem** pointing down or up.

 This is a **crotchet rest** (or quarter note rest). Remember, rests are silences that occur in music. A crotchet rest is also worth **one beat** of the pulse.

Tracks 8 & 9

Jimitator

Start ..../..../....

End ..../..../....

This piece makes use of crotchets and crotchet rests. Make sure you are playing in time with the pulse.

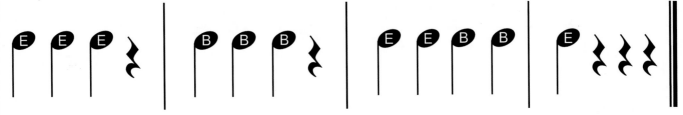

play piece 4 times

Profile

Jimi Hendrix
1942-1970

James Marshall Hendrix was born in Seattle, Washington but moved to London in 1966 where he found fame with his brand of Blues-influenced Rock music. He played the guitar left-handed but mainly used a right-handed Fender Stratocaster upside down with the strings reversed. His innovative use of guitar effects as well as experimental studio work meant that he would take electric guitar playing to a different level. His live shows would often incorporate displays of showmanship such as playing the guitar behind his head, behind his back and even with his teeth but it was ultimately his incredible guitar work that will ensure that he goes down in history as arguably the most influential Rock guitarist of all time.

Playlist - Voodoo Child (Slight Return), All Along The Watchtower, Little Wing

Cat Got The Cream

Start ..../..../....
End ..../..../....

Time Signatures

The two number fours at the start of the piece are called the **time signature** (or meter). This tells us how many beats are in a bar of music. This time signature tells us that there are four crotchet beats in a bar.

four ——— 4

crotchets ——— 4
(quarter notes)

The time signature can be viewed as a fraction and therefore seen as **four quarter notes** (or crotchets) in a bar. Listen out for the introduction at the beginning of this song.

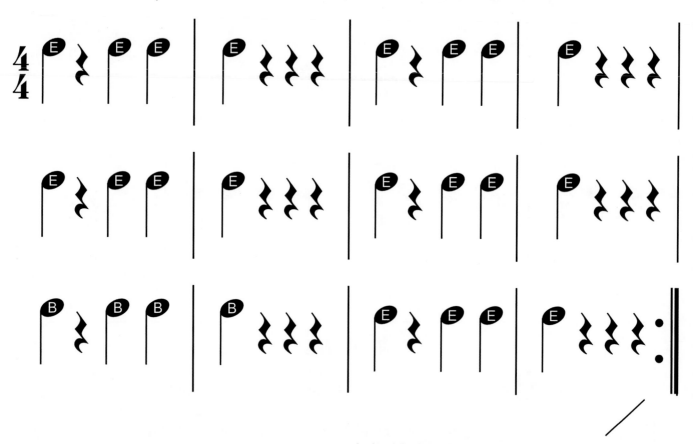

A double bar line with two dots tells us to go back to the beginning of the piece of music. This is called the **repeat sign**.

8

Nearly Varna

Start ..../..../....

End ..../..../....

This piece can be played as written or if you want, you can let the notes ring to give it a different feel. Try playing the first two times quietly and then the last two times loudly. Listen out for the introduction played on the guitar.

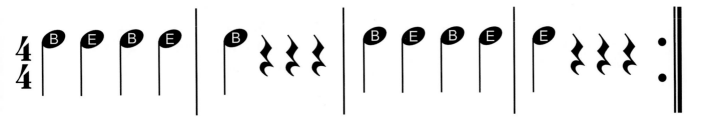

Play piece 4 times

Practising

- In order to make good progress on your guitar, it is essential that you practise. If you get into good habits right from the start, your playing will improve more quickly.

- Listen to what you are playing. This may sound obvious, but it is important that you are aware of what you are playing as well as making sure you are in time with the backing track.

- Make time for practice and practise often. It is better to divide your practice time up into small manageable sessions rather than one big one with a long gap before the next time you play. This will help your fingers (as well as your brain) to learn and remember.

- Practise the things you know as well as the things you aren't yet familiar with. Once you have learnt a piece of music, don't forget about it, revisit it as often as you can.

- Don't worry about making mistakes. Every mistake you make will ultimately help you in the long run.

Summary

In this lesson we have learnt how to:

- Read crotchets and crotchet rests.
- Identify time signatures.
- Identify repeat marks.

Things To Remember

- Make sure you are holding your plectrum correctly.
- Listen to the recording and try to play along with the track.
- Be aware of the rests as well as the notes.

Pitch

Pitch is a musical word that is used to describe high and low sounds. Of the two notes that we have already learnt, E has a higher pitch than B.

The stave is a set of five horizontal lines on which we write music.

At the beginning of the stave, we place a **treble clef**. This tells us that this music can be played on the guitar.

Every note has its own place on the stave. The **E note** is at the top of the stave in the space between the two uppermost lines.

The **B note** is written on the middle line. Note stems can point upwards or downwards.

Tracks 14 & 15

Blue and Pink

Start ..../..../....

End ..../..../....

Remember, the higher the pitch of a note, the higher on the musical stave it is placed. The direction **x4** written above the end repeat indicates that the whole piece is played **four times** in total.

The G Note

The next piece introduces a new note. The **G** is found on **string 3**. It is a lower pitched note than both E and B and is written on the **second line** of the stave. Remember, note stems can point both upwards or downwards. We play our G note in exactly the same way as both our E and B.

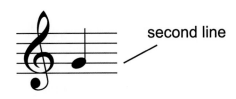

second line

Tracks 16 & 17

Zero Hour

Start ..../..../....

End ..../..../....

This piece makes use of the G, B and E notes. Make sure you count the rests. Because the music is written on several lines, it has bar numbers at the beginning of each line to help with practice.

Profile

Eddie Van Halen
b1955

Eddie Van Halen was born in The Netherlands but moved to California with his family when he was seven years old. Eddie and his brother Alex both took piano lessons from an early age but it was first the drums and then the guitar that he became interested in. Although he wasn't the first to use it, Eddie's incorporation of right-handed tapping techniques along with his use of speed picking and memorable guitar riffs have become his trademarks. His influence on Rock guitar playing, especially during the 1980s, has led him to be considered by some polls as the greatest guitarist of all time.

Playlist - Eruption, Jump, Panama

11

The Field

This piece is a bit of a challenge. Just as we did with "Nearly Varna", try to play this one with the notes left to ring to give the piece a different quality. The letters *D.C.* tell us to repeat the piece of music from the beginning. The letters stand for *da capo* which is an Italian term meaning 'from the beginning'. In this instance, we have to use *D.C.* to go back to the beginning of the piece because we have already used the repeat sign at the end of bar 4.

Note Reminder

E   B   G

When reading music, try to spot patterns. Look at the way the notes are moving. Are they moving upwards or downwards or staying on the same note? Lots of pieces use repetition or may have passages that are the same as previous sections with just a few altered notes.

Summary

In this lesson we have learnt how to:

- Read notes on the stave.
- Identify and play our G on the third string.
- Identify *D.C.* and understand what it means.

Things To Remember

- Make sure you are playing in time with the pulse.
- The higher pitched a note is, the higher it is written on the stave.
- Note stems can go upwards or downwards.

Duration

Up to now, we have used crotchets (quarter notes) and crotchet rests (quarter note rests) to play our pieces. As we know, crotchets last for one beat each. In order for us to create and play more interesting rhythms, we need to use notes and rests that are longer and shorter than crotchets. The length of any given note is known as the **duration**.

The Minim

 This note is called a **minim** (or half note). It lasts for **two beats** of the pulse. Like a crotchet, its stem can point down or up.

 This is a **minim rest** (or half note rest). Like the crotchet rest, it is a silence that occurs in music. The minim rest also lasts for **two beats** of the pulse. It sits on top of the third line of the stave.

Tracks 20 & 21

Martian Rocks

Start ..../..../....

End ..../..../....

This piece uses our E, B and G strings and is made up of minims and minim rests. The numbers underneath the notes are there to help you count along with the pulse. Watch out for the repeat!

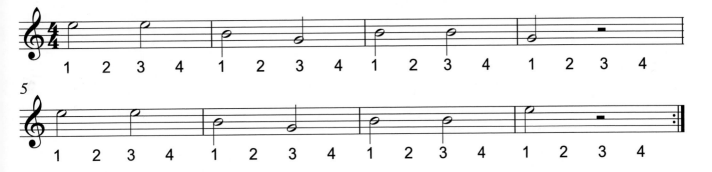

Monkey Town

This piece uses a mixture of G, B and E notes as well as crotchets, minims and minim rests. It is important that you pay particular attention when moving between the second E note in bar 6 and the G at the beginning of bar 7. Remember, the numbers written underneath the stave are there to help you count. Listen out for the bass guitar on the recording before the melody begins.

Tracks 24 & 25

Northern Soul

Watch out for the repeat at the end of the first line and the *D.C.* (*da capo*) marking at the end. Remember, this tells us to play the piece again from the beginning.

Summary

In this lesson we have learnt how to:

• Identify and play minims and minim rests.
• Play pieces with mixed E, B and G strings.
• Play pieces with mixed crotchets and minims.

Things To Remember

• Count in time with the pulse of the piece of music you are playing along with.
• Rest your picking hand on the bridge of your guitar. This will help you to find your strings without looking.

The Fretting Hand

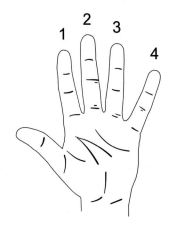

In order to play more notes, we have to use the fingers on our **fretting hand**. We number our fretting hand fingers 1 to 4 from our index finger through to our little finger.

The A Note

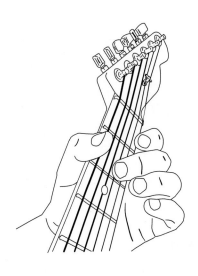

With the tip of the **second finger** on your fretting hand, press down **string 3** at **fret 2** as demonstrated in the picture. Remember, frets are the metal wires that are found underneath the strings on the front of the neck of the guitar. It is important to make sure your thumb is at a right angle to the neck of your guitar. Whilst you hold the string down, play it with your plectrum in the same way as we have played the other notes that we have learnt up to now. This new note is called **A**. It is higher in pitch than our G.

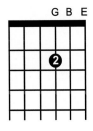

In order to make sure that you don't get any buzzes or dead notes, it is important to use your fingertip to press down the string as near to the metal fret-wire as possible. We can use this diagram to show where our note A is. The horizontal lines represent the frets whilst the vertical lines represent the strings. The black circle shows you where to press the string down and the number in the circle tells you which fretting hand finger to use.

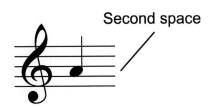

Second space

On the stave, the A note is placed in the **second space** in between the G and B notes. The stem of the A note points **upwards**.

DiY

Start ..../..../....

End ..../..../....

This piece is made up entirely of A notes. Make sure you follow the rhythm closely and listen out for the introduction.

x4

The Fortress

Tracks 28 & 29

Start ..../..../....

End ..../..../....

This piece uses A and G notes. Remember, A and G notes are found on the same string. It is important to keep your finger close to the string when lifting it off to play your G note. Watch out for the repeat at the end of bar 8.

Backyard Rock

Tracks 30 & 31

Start ..../..../....

End ..../..../....

This piece uses B, A and G notes. Make sure you play the correct rhythm and watch out for the minim rest in bar 4.

x4

Summary

In this lesson we have learnt how to:

- Correctly number our fretting hand fingers.
- Identify and play our fretted A note on string 3.
- Play pieces with mixed B, A and G notes.

Things To Remember

- Use the tip of your finger to fret the note.
- Press the string down as near to the fret as possible.
- Listen out for buzzes when you are playing the A.

Tablature (or **TAB** for short) is a form of musical notation that we can use to help us play the guitar. Guitar TAB is written specifically for the guitar and uses lines and numbers to indicate where a particular note is on your instrument. TAB is a very useful tool as it enables us to play notes anywhere on the guitar and is usually used in conjunction with **standard notation** that we have already been learning.

The TAB stave uses six horizontal lines. Each line represents a guitar string. The three strings that we have already looked at are indicated in the following diagram.

```
E _____
B _____
G _____
  _____
  _____
  _____
```

The letters TAB are placed at the start of a tablature stave.

```
T _____
A _____
B _____
```

Numbers are then placed on the stave to indicate which string to play. An **open string** (a string that is played without using your fretting hand such as our E, B & G notes) is represented by a zero. This TAB is telling us to play our **open G string**.

```
T _____
A ____0_____
B _____
```

Fretted notes (notes that use our fretting hand to press down a string) are indicated using the number of the fret that you are to press down. This would be how we show our **A note**.

```
T _____
A ____2_____
B _____
```

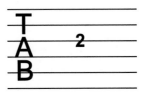

Dick Dale
1937-2019

Dick Dale was nicknamed "King of the Surf Guitar" and with his Middle Eastern influenced melodies, fast single note picking technique and use of reverb effects he created the archetypal Surf Guitar sound. Dale played the guitar left-handed and used a right-handed Fender Stratocaster which he turned upside down without altering the order of the strings meaning the low E string was nearest to the floor. Dale's music still remains popular and his style has influenced musicians as varied as Jimi Hendrix, The Ramones and Van Halen.

Playlist - Miserlou, King of the Surf Guitar, Nitro

Desert Rock

Desert rock uses A notes and G notes. The piece of music is written out in both TAB and standard notation and both staves are joined together using a **bracke**t. When more than one stave is joined to another, it is called a **system**.

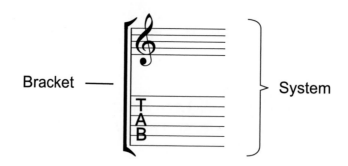

Bracket ———   System

In order to make sure that we play the correct rhythm, we need to read both staves. Make sure you count the rests in bars 2, 4, 6 and 8.

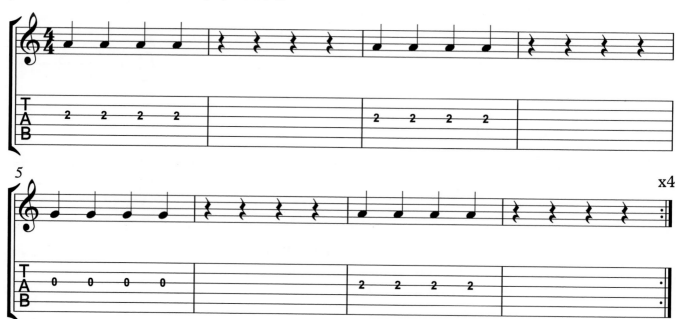

Profile

Chet Atkins
1924-2001
Born Chester Burton Atkins in Tennessee, Chet Atkins' use of a thumbpick and fingers meant he could play both melody and bass parts simultaneously and his Jazz-influenced Country style helped to establish the Nashville sound that subsequently became a huge influence on early Rock 'n' Roll. in 2016, Atkins was ranked number 21 on the Rolling Stone's list of "The 100 Greatest Guitarists Of All Time".

Playlist - Mister Sandman, Freight Train, Black Mountain Rag

The Semibreve

o This note is called a **semibreve** (or whole note). It has no stem and lasts for **four beats** of the pulse.

This is a **semibreve rest** (or whole note rest). It hangs underneath the fourth line of the stave and also lasts for **four beats** of the pulse.

Tracks 34 & 35

Listen Up

Start ..../..../....

End ..../..../....

This piece uses Semibreves in bars 2, 4 and 6. Make sure you let these notes ring for their full values and watch for the rests at the end of bar 8. Remember, the numbers underneath the notation are there to help with counting.

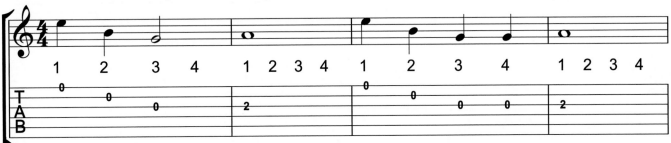

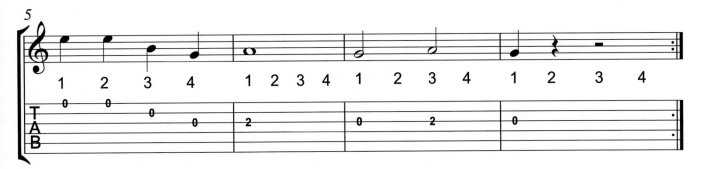

Carlos Santana
b1947

Profile

Santana was born in Mexico but moved to San Francisco at a young age where was taught the guitar by his father who was a Mariachi musician. His big breakthrough was in 1969 where his band performed their blend of Rock and Latin American influenced music at the Woodstock Festival. Throughout his career, he has used Gibson and Yamaha guitars but it is his association with Paul Reed Smith guitars since 1982 that he is best known.

Playlist - Oye Como Va, She's Not There, Smooth

Heavy Balloon

Start ..../..../....

End ..../..../....

Listen out for the introduction at the start of the piece. The guitar begins after the drum fill. Remember, rests are silences in music so make sure you pay particular attention to the rests throughout the piece as well as the repeat sign at the end of bar 4.

Jimmy Page
b1944

During the 1960s, Jimmy Page cut his teeth as a session musician in London working with acts such as The Rolling Stones, The Kinks and The Who but he is remembered principally for his work with the Rock group Led Zeppelin. Page is responsible for writing many of the group's earlier works and his heavy riffs along with his eclectic soloing and clever use of altered tuning gave Led Zeppelin a sound that would influence artists as diverse as Queen, The Ramones, Foo Fighters, Red Hot Chili Peppers and The Beastie Boys.

Playlist - Dazed and Confused, Black Dog, Stairway to Heaven.

Summary

In this lesson we have learnt how to:

• Read Guitar Tablature.
• Identify and play semibreves and semibreve rests.
• Play pieces with mixed crotchets, minims and semibreves.

Things To Remember

• Be aware of rests and note lengths when playing your pieces.
• Let your longer notes ring for their full values.
• Try to read both the tab and standard notation.

A New Note

The D Note

We are going to learn a new note. The **D** is written on the **fourth line** of the stave. The stem of the D note points **downwards**.

This note can be found on **string 2**, **fret 3** and we play it using the **third finger** on our fretting hand.

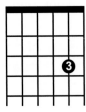

Tracks 38 & 39

Thrill Seeker

Start ..../..../....

End ..../..../....

This piece makes use of our new note D. Watch out for the repeat sign at the end of bar 8. At the beginning of bar 9, there is a **start repeat sign**. This indicates the start of a section that is to be repeated. The **end repeat sign** in bar 16 indicates that we are to go back to bar 9 and play that section again. We also make use of **semibreve rests** in bars 2, 4 and 6. Remember, rests are silences that occur in music.

Start repeat sign

End repeat sign

21

Tracks 40 & 41

The Bomb

Start ..../..../....

End ..../..../....

This piece uses B, D and E notes. On the first time, play the piece as written. During the second playing, you can make up your own piece of music using the B, D and E notes. This is called an **improvisation**. So long as you stick to these three notes, you can play anything you want. Listen to the improvised solo on the recorded version for some ideas. On the third time through, repeat the melody as written. The piece begins with a crotchet rest before the first note, so the count in is **1 2 3 4 rest**...

improvising

• Don't be scared to play the same note or phrase more than once. Repetition can be a good thing when improvising.

• Leaving space between notes can be very effective. Don't feel like you have to fill up the music with lots and lots of notes.

• Try to mix long notes and short notes to make your playing more rhythmically interesting.

• Remember, so long as you use the correct notes, you can play whatever you like and it will sound right.

The Dotted Minim

 This is a **dotted minim** (or dotted half note). It lasts for **three beats** of the pulse.

 This is a **dotted minim** rest (or dotted half note rest). It also lasts for **three beats** of the pulse.

Tracks 42 & 43

Floydian Slip

Start ..../..../....

End ..../..../....

The notes G, A, B, D and E are all used in this piece. It has a fairly slow pulse so make sure you let the notes ring for their full values. The symbol ⌒ over the final note is called a **fermata**. This indicates that you are to hold the note for longer than its normal value. Remember to use the second finger for your A note and the third finger for your D note

Summary

In this lesson we have learnt how to:

• Read and play our D note on string 2.
• Identify and play dotted minims and dotted minim rests.
• Play pieces with mixed crotchets, minims, dotted minims and semibreves.
• Identify and understand the fermata.

Things To Remember

• Try not to look at your hands when playing.
• Use the tips of your fingers when fretting notes and make sure you use the correct fingers.
• Press the string down as near to the fret as possible.

23

The Pentatonic Scale

The High G Note

The **high G** sits on the **top line** of the stave. Its stem points **downwards**.

We use our **third finger** to play this note and it can be found on **string 1 fret 3**. We have already learnt an open G on string 3. This G has a higher pitch.

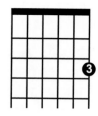

First and Second Time Bars

Sometimes a passage of music may have two different endings. Rather than write out the same passage twice, we can use repeat markings and special brackets to indicate the two endings. We call these **first and second time bars** or **first and second endings**.

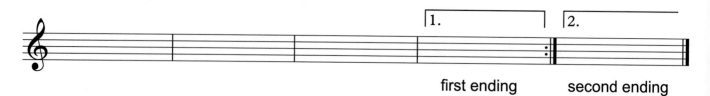

first ending   second ending

In the example above, on the first time through, you play up to bar 4 and then return to the first bar as directed by the repeat mark. On the second playing, you play up to bar 3, miss out bar 4 and go straight to bar 5.

Profile

Kurt Cobain
1967-1994

During the short period of time with his work in the Grunge band Nirvana, Cobain redefined the sound of 90s Rock music. Without any formal tuition, Cobain's raw and aggressive guitar style was the antithesis to the trend of technically proficient playing that was prevalent at the time and subsequently influenced a generation of guitarists. Cobain played guitar left-handed and favoured Fender guitars, especially Stratocasters, Telecasters, Jaguars and Mustangs.

Playlist - Smells Like Teen Spirit, In Bloom, Heart Shaped Box

Cradle To Grave

The opening section of this piece uses first and second time bars. Watch out for the repeated passage between bars 10 and 16. The piece is made up entirely of E and G notes using mixed crotchets, minims, dotted minims and semibreves.

Entrance

This piece uses B, D, E and G notes and a first and second ending. Watch out for the four-bar first ending and the two bar repeated passage at the very end. The guitar begins after the drum fill.

Tony Iommi
b1948

Despite an industrial injury that meant he lost the tips of the second and third fingers of his fretting hand, Toni Iommi's heavy distortion-laden riffs with the band Black Sabbath became the blueprint for Heavy Metal music. Iommi detuned his guitar to help him bend the strings and as a result, the darker sound that was produced helped to define his style. As a left-hander, throughout his career, Iommi has mainly favoured SG style guitars.

Playlist - Iron Man, Paranoid, Supernaut

If we put all the notes that we have learnt together, we have a **scale**. This scale is made up of five different notes; G, A, B, D and E (plus the high G) and is called the **G major pentatonic**. It can be used to create pieces of music and for improvising. It is a good idea to practise the notes from the scale before attempting the next piece. If we do this, our fingers will become more accustomed to the scale shape and in turn, this will make the piece easier to play.

Listen to how the notes go higher in pitch when you play from the lowest to the highest note (ascending). Try playing the notes in reverse order as well (descending).

Tracks 48 & 49

Tiny Bird

Start ..../..../....

End ..../..../....

This piece uses the G major pentatonic scale both ascending and descending and is played at a slow tempo so remember to count and try not to rush.

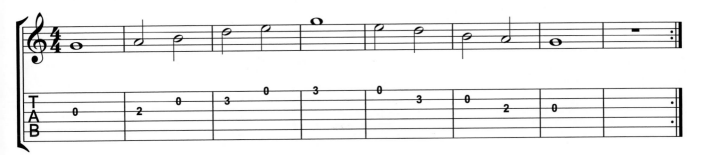

Summary

In this lesson we have learnt how to:

• Read and play our G note on string 1.
• Identify and understand first and second time bars.
• Play a G major pentatonic scale.

Things To Remember

• Practise playing the G major pentatonic scale both ascending and descending.
• Make sure you are using the correct fretting hand fingers.
• Don't forget to revisit pieces from the book that you have already learnt.

First Position

In this lesson, we will look at the notes in **first position** on strings 1, 2 and 3. Positions on the guitar are determined by the location of the first finger of the fretting hand. First position simply means that:

- Notes on **fret 1** are played with the **first finger**.
- Notes on **fret 2** are played with the **second finger**.
- Notes on **fret 3** are played with the **third finger**.
- Notes on **fret 4** are played with the **fourth finger**.

The F Note

This note is called **F**. It is written on the **fifth line** of the stave. The stem of the F note points **downwards**.

The F is played by the **first finger**, on the **first fret** of the **first string**.

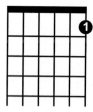

Tracks 50 & 51

Point Break

Start ..../..../....

End ..../..../....

This piece is composed entirely of E, F and G notes on string 1. Remember to stay in first position and watch out for the repeat.

keep your first finger on

Top Tip

When moving from your F to your G, you can keep your first finger on fret 1. That way, when you play the F again in the following bar, you can just lift your third finger off the G on fret 3 and your F note will already be there. Playing any note on a higher fret cancels out the note on the lower fret behind it.

The C Note

The C is written in the **third space** of the stave. The stem of the C note points **downwards**.

The C is played by the **first finger**, on the **first fret** of the **second string**.

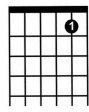

🔊 **Tracks 52 & 53**

Scoville

Start ..../..../....

End ..../..../....

This piece uses our new C note as well as B and D. Watch out for the rests and don't forget to repeat the piece.

First Position Notes On The Treble Strings

Just as we did with our G Major Pentatonic scale in Lesson 8, we can play the first position notes on the treble (thinnest) strings as an exercise to help us learn where they can be found on the fretboard. It is important to bear in mind that notes in music are set out in alphabetical order. The musical alphabet uses seven letters from A through to G and then begins again.

Windy City

Start ..../..../....

End ..../..../....

In this piece, we use all the notes that we have learnt up to now. Remember to use the correct fingers and watch out for the minims in bars 4 and 8 and the semibreve in bar 12. See if you can spot any repeated bars or phrases.

Summary

In this lesson we have learnt how to:

- Play the first position notes on the treble strings.
- Identify and play both the F on string 1 and the C on string 2.

Things To Remember

- Practise playing the first position notes both ascending and descending.
- Make sure you are using the correct fretting hand fingers.
- Try not to look at your hands when playing.

Lesson 10

Low Notes

The Bottom E

The thickest string on the guitar is the sixth string and is called **E**. It is lower in pitch than the open E on the first string. Listen to the E on string 6 and then the E on string 1. They are both E notes but the first string has a higher pitch than the sixth string.

This is how the low E note looks on the stave. Remember, the higher the pitch of a note, the higher on the stave it is written. The lower the pitch of a note, the lower it is written. In the case of our low E, we have to draw extra lines called **ledger lines** because the pitch of the low E is below the bottom line of the stave. Our low E is the lowest pitched note we can play on the guitar and is sometimes referred to as the **bottom E**.

Tracks 56 & 57

Tombstone Grit

Start ..../..../....

End ..../..../....

This piece is composed entirely of Low E notes. Make sure you pay particular attention to the rhythm on the standard notation stave. The guitar starts after the drum fill.

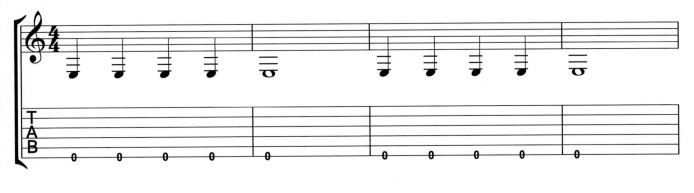

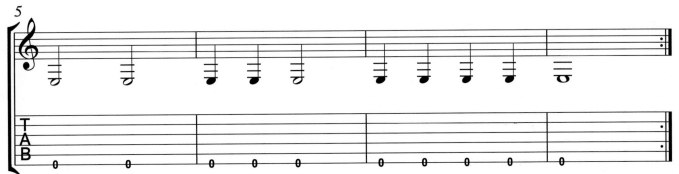

31

Quavers

Two **quavers** (eighth notes) joined together by a beam last for **one beat** of the pulse and can be written with their stems pointing upwards or downwards.

The Low G Note

The **low G** is written below the **second ledger line** underneath the stave. The stem of the Low G note points **upwards**.

The low G note is found on **string 6**, **fret 3** and we use the **third finger** on our fretting hand to play this note.

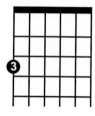

Tracks 58 & 59

Green Noise

Start ..../..../....
End ..../..../....

The numbers underneath the standard notation stave are there to help you count. Even though the pulse is still counted as **1, 2, 3, 4,** there are 'ands' (**&**) added in between each beat to help us count the quavers. In doing this, we split each beat into two equal parts. This is called **two-part counting**.

This piece uses **low E** and **G** notes and also has a tempo marking (♩=100) to indicate how fast it is to be performed. In this case, it is to be played at 100 beats per minute (100 bpm).

The Low F Note

The **low F** is written on the **third ledger line** underneath the stave. The stem of the Low F note points **upwards**.

The low F note is found on **string 6**, **fret 1** and we use the **first finger** on our fretting hand to play this note.

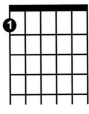

When we play our low notes, it is important that we use the correct fretting hand thumb position. Make sure your thumb is placed halfway down and at a right angle to the neck of the guitar as indicated in the diagram.

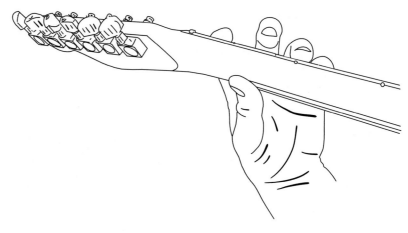

Tracks 60 & 61

Dream State

Start ..../..../....

End ..../..../....

This piece uses E, F and G notes on the low E string. Make sure you count the dotted minims correctly and let the notes ring for their full values. It is essential at this stage that you use your first finger for fret 1 and your third finger for fret 3. It is also important to note that the four quavers that are beamed together in bar 3 are played in exactly the same way as two sets of double quavers would be.

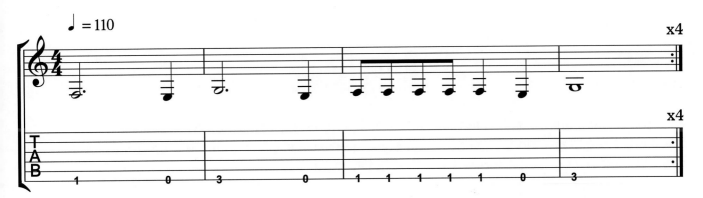

Summary

In this lesson we have learnt how to:

- Identify and play our low E string and the low F and G notes on string 6.
- Play pieces using quavers.
- Identify and understand tempo markings.

Things To Remember

- Try not to look at your picking hand.
- Make sure you are using the correct fretting hand fingers.
- Use two-part counting when playing a piece that contains quavers.

33

The A String

The Open A Note

The **fifth string** is called **A**. It is lower in pitch than the A that we have already learnt on fret 2 of our third string. This is how the low A note looks on the stave. The low A note is found on the **second ledger line**.

Tracks 62 & 63

Sand Dune

Start ..../..../....

End ..../..../....

This piece uses our open A string as well as E and G from string 6. Watch out for the repeat at the end of bar 4.

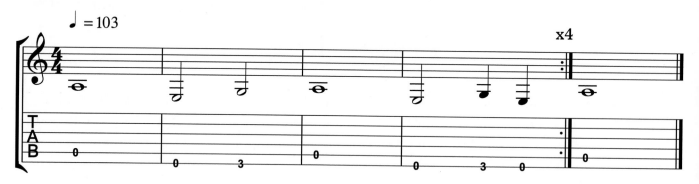

Tracks 64 & 65

Billy Rock

Start ..../..../....

End ..../..../....

This piece uses our open A string as well as E, F and G from string 6. As well as a tempo marking, there is also an indication of the style in which the piece is to be performed. In this case, the piece is to be performed in a Rockabilly style.

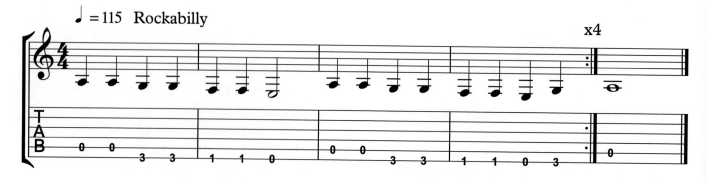

Red Lines

In this piece, we use quavers, crotchets, minims and semibreves. Just like Billy Rock, this piece is composed entirely of A, G, F and E notes. Try to keep your first finger on the F whilst playing the G in bar 4 - remember your thumb position that we looked at before we learnt our low F note. During the introduction, the bass guitar plays the melody once on its own and then once with the drums. Watch out for the repeat of the first line.

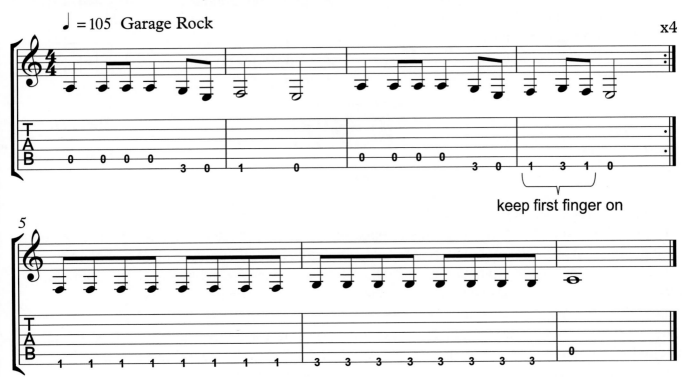

keep first finger on

John Frusciante

b1970

John Frusciante is best known for his work with the Los Angeles based Funk Rock band, Red Hot Chili Peppers. His wide range of influences means that he is at home playing complex Jimi Hendrix influenced rhythm parts, funky riffs or soaring lead lines. His main guitar is his 1962 Fender Stratocaster given to him by Red Hot Chili Peppers frontman Anthony Kiedis.

Playlist - Under The Bridge, Californication, By The Way

Summary

In this lesson we have learnt how to:

- Identify and play our A on string 5.
- Play pieces using mixed A, G, F and E notes.
- Identify and understand style markings.

Things To Remember

- Fret the notes with the tips of your fingers.
- Rest your picking hand on the bridge of your guitar.
- Listen out for buzzing or dead notes.

Notes On The A String

The Low B Note

This is our **low B** note. The low B hangs underneath the **first ledger line** beneath the stave. Its stem points **upwards**.

We have already learnt an open B on string 2. This B has a lower pitch. We play this note with the **second finger** on our fretting hand.

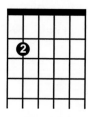

Tracks 68 & 69

Start ..../..../....

End ..../..../....

FM Radio

Counting

This piece is made up entirely of B and A notes on string 5. The first two bars are repeated eight times in total. Sometimes music contains repeated sections and although it seems quite an easy task at first, keeping track of how many repeats you have played can be a bit of a challenge. In this piece, you are having to count more than one thing at once. You have to keep count of how many B notes you have played before you change to an A note as well as making sure you repeat this pattern a total of eight times. As you can see, there are fourteen B notes before you play the open A, but it is quite easy to lose count when you are concentrating on other things. A useful technique is to use words or phrases to help you. It doesn't matter how silly the phrase is (sometimes the sillier the better!) providing the words fit. For example, you could count the piece below using the names of famous guitarists - One Frank Zappa, Jimi Hendrix, Eric Clapton, Jimmy Page, Two Frank Zappa, Jimi Hendrix, Eric Clapton, Jimmy Page and so on.

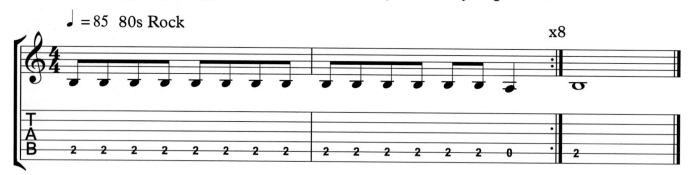

Brian May
b1947
As guitarist and songwriter in the band Queen, Brian May has written and performed some of the most recognisable songs in the history of Rock. A lot of May's unmistakable tone can be contributed to Red Special, the guitar that he built with the help of his father whilst still at school. May's melodic approach to soloing and clever use of overdubbed guitar harmonies gave Queen a unique sound that has influenced countless bands since.
Playlist - Bohemian Rhapsody, Brighton Rock, Killer Queen

Lost and Found

This piece uses low E and G as well as the A and B notes found on string 5. Make sure you pay particular attention to the rests found in the first four bars.

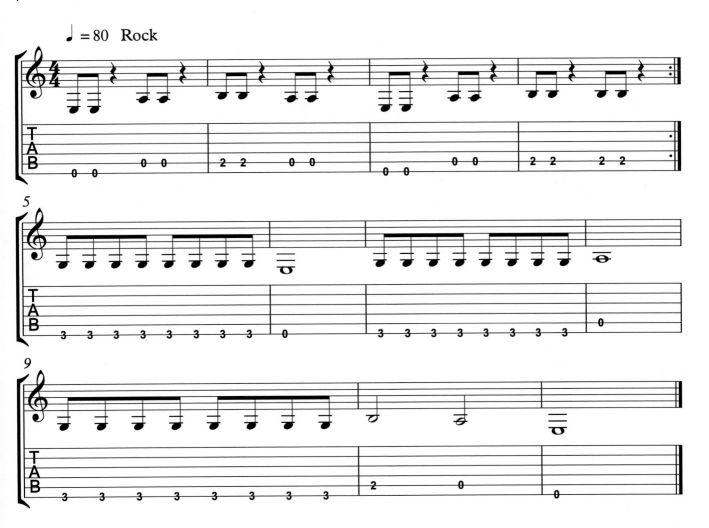

The Low C Note

The low C sits on the **first ledger line** beneath the stave. Its stem points **upwards**.

This note is found on **fret 3 of string 5** and is played with our **third finger**.

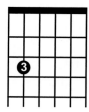

Tracks 72 & 73

Skank it

Start ..../..../....

End ..../..../....

This piece uses A and C from string 5 as well as E and G from string 6. Watch out for the repeats on both lines and the *D.C.* at the end of bar 8. The guitar begins after the drum fill.

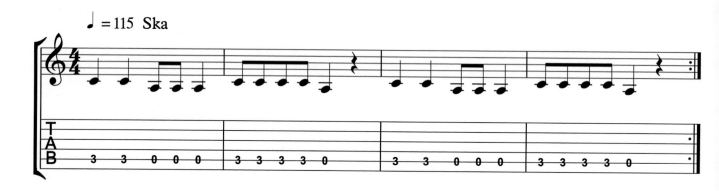

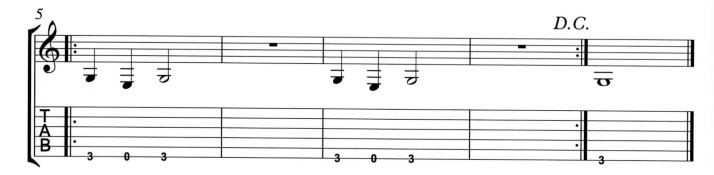

Summary

In this lesson we have learnt how to:

- Identify and play our B and C notes on string 5.
- Play pieces using mixed notes on strings 5 and 6.

Things To Remember

- Make sure you use the correct fretting hand fingers.
- Remember to play along with the backing tracks.
- Look at the music, not your hands.

38

The D String

The Open D String

The **open D** note is found on string 4 and hangs underneath the stave. Its stem points **upwards**. This D is lower in pitch than the D found on fret 3 of string 2.

Tracks 74 & 75

Fonkey

Start ..../..../....

End ..../..../....

This piece is made up entirely of open D notes. Make sure you play the correct rhythm and observe the rests and repeat mark. The two ➤ markings at the end of bar 3 are called **accents** and indicate that these notes are to be played with more force than the rest of the notes in the piece.

The E Note

This **E note** sits on the **first line** of the stave. Its stem points **upwards**.

This **E note** is found on **fret 2** of our **fourth string**. We now know three E notes. Play each of them and listen to how they sound the same but at different pitches.

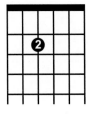

Tracks 76 & 77

Assembly

Start ..../..../....

End ..../..../....

The notes D and E are used in this piece. Make sure you pay particular attention to the quaver rhythm in bars 2 and 4.

The F Note

This is our **F note**. It is found in the first space of the stave.

The F is found on **fret 3 of our fourth string**. We play this note with the **third finger** of our fretting hand.

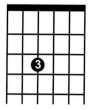

Tracks 78 & 79

Airship

Start ..../..../....

End ..../..../....

This piece is composed entirely of D, E and F notes. Make sure you pay particular attention to the rhythm that is repeated throughout bars 1 to 8 and bars 17 to 20.

Summary

In this lesson we have learnt how to:

- Identify and play our D, E and F notes on string 4.
- Play pieces using accented notes

Things To Remember

- Make sure you read the rhythms and stay in time with the pulse.
- Use the correct fretting hand fingers.
- Rest your picking hand on the bridge of the guitar and concentrate on the music.

Syncopation

Single quavers (eighth notes) last for **half a beat** of the pulse and can be written with their stems pointing upwards or downwards.

This is a **quaver rest** (eighth note rest). Remember, rests are **periods of silence** in music. A quaver rest also lasts for **half a beat** of the pulse.

Take a look at this rhythm.

If we were to take away the second note in this bar, the rhythm would look like this.

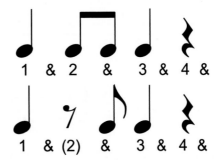

We treat both these rhythms the same, but instead of playing the first quaver of beat 2, we substitute it for a rest. It is important to make sure that we feel where the rest is and be aware of the pulse. Rhythms that are unexpected or have off-beat accents like the example above are called **syncopated rhythms**. At first, rhythms like this may feel a little strange, but with practice, they will become more familiar.

Tracks 80 & 81

Tangled

Start ..../..../....
End ..../..../....

This track uses the syncopated rhythm that you can see above. Make sure you play the two bars at the start of the piece four times. The guitar part starts after the drum fill.

41

The E Minor Pentatonic Scale

In bars 7 and 8 of the following piece, we play a new scale. The scale is an **E minor pentatonic** scale. The notation and tablature below show the scale in its descending form, but remember to play the notes in ascending order as well. Just like we did in Tiny Bird, practise the notes from this scale to help you play the piece.

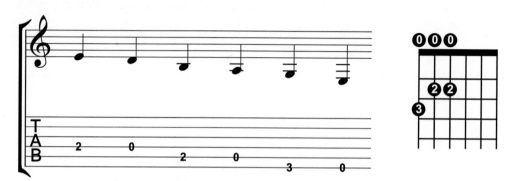

Tracks 82 & 83

Lemon Sherbet

Start ..../..../....

End ..../..../....

In this piece, we use another syncopated rhythm. Remember to feel where the rest is and listen to the recording to get an idea of how the rhythm sounds. This piece also makes use of **D.C. al Fine**. *Fine* is the Italian word for 'end' or 'ending'. Remember that **D.C.** (*da capo*) means 'from the beginning', so **D.C. al Fine** tells us to repeat the piece from the beginning up to the word Fine.

42

Mrs Hippie

Start ..../..../....
End ..../..../....

This piece uses a syncopated rhythm in bars 1 and 3 and is composed entirely of notes from the E minor pentatonic scale we learnt earlier in this lesson. Just as we did with The Bomb in Lesson 7, on the first time, play the piece as written. During the second playing, use the E minor pentatonic scale to improvise a solo. Remember to listen to the improvised solo on the recorded version for some ideas. On the third time through, repeat the melody as written.

Profile

Robert Johnson
1911-1938

Although much of his life is shrouded in mystery, Robert Johnson is widely regarded as one of the most important Blues musicians of all time. The legend that he sold his soul to the devil in exchange for mastery of the guitar has helped to reinforce his notoriety. Between 1936 and 1937 he recorded twenty-nine songs which continue to inspire and captivate listeners to this day and has influenced musicians including Bob Dylan, Eric Clapton, Keith Richards and Muddy Waters. Johnson was inducted into the Rock & Roll Hall of Fame in 1986.

Playlist- Hellhound On My Trail, Cross Road Blues, I Believe I'll Dust My Broom

Summary

In this lesson we have learnt how to:

- Understand and play three pieces using syncopated rhythms.
- Play pieces of music that use *D.C. al Fine* markings.
- Play the E Minor Pentatonic scale and use it to improvise a solo.

Things To Remember

- Make sure you are aware of the pulse when playing.
- Feel where the rests are when playing syncopated rhythms.
- When improvising, so long as you use the correct notes, you can play what you want and it will sound right.

Tied Notes

We can join two notes of the same pitch together to make one long note. Notes are joined together using a curved line called a **tie**. This means that we can play notes that last for longer than four beats, or notes that begin in one bar and end in another.

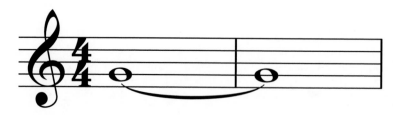

In the above example, the G note lasts for eight beats (four plus four). We play the first note and let it ring for the duration of both notes.

Tracks 86 & 87

Amulet

Start ..../..../....

End ..../..../....

This piece uses tied notes throughout. Make sure you let the notes ring for their full value and watch out for the rest in bar 16.

♩ = 135   Blues Rock

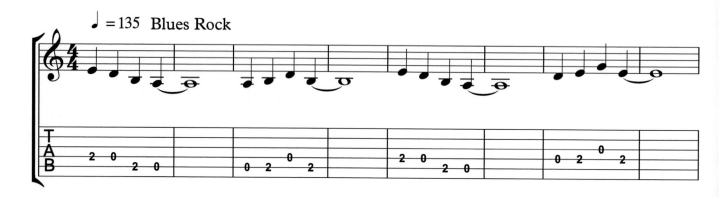

Return of Amulet

Start ..../..../....

End ..../..../....

In this piece, we play the same notes as Amulet, only at a higher pitch. We can say that we are playing the piece an **octave** higher. The notes sound the same but higher. As a challenge, try to play the piece the first time in the low octave (as in Amulet) and then on the repeat, play the piece as written below. Or alternatively, start in the high octave and then play the repeat in the low octave.

Look at the notes in this scale. It is a repeating pattern and contains notes both from the **E minor pentatonic scale** - E G A B D E (which we used in Lemon Sherbet, Mrs Hippie, Amulet and Return Of Amulet from Lessons 14 and 15) and the **G major pentatonic scale** - G A B D E G (which we learnt in Tiny Bird from Lesson 8).

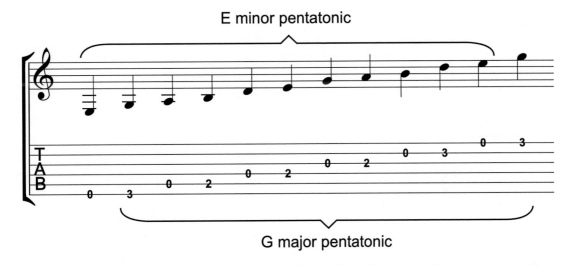

As you can see, both scales contain the same notes, but the starting note, or the **root note**, is different. Because of this, the two scales have a different quality. We refer to this as the **tonality**.

i Will Follow

Start ..../..../....

End ..../..../....

This piece uses notes from a **two octave G major pentatonic scale**. Pay particular attention when skipping strings such as the D at the end of bar 2 to the G at the beginning of bar 3. Remember to rest your picking hand to help you find the string you are playing.

♩ = 140 Garage Rock

Summary

In this lesson we have learnt how to:

- Understand and play tied notes.
- Play pieces of music that use two octave major and minor pentatonic scales.
- Understand tonality.

Things To Remember

- Let notes ring for their full value.
- Try not to look at your hands when playing the guitar, concentrate on reading the music.
- Play the pieces with the backing tracks.

Power Chords

In this lesson, we are going to focus on how to play **power chords**. In order to do this, we need to learn how to play two strings simultaneously with our picking hand.

🔊

Tracks 92 & 93

Doom

Start ..../..../....

End ..../..../....

On the standard notation and TAB stave, the open A and E notes are stacked on top of each other. This tells us that these two notes are to be played at the same time. Remember to rest your picking hand on your bridge and let the plectrum play through both strings. This action is also referred to as a **double stop**.

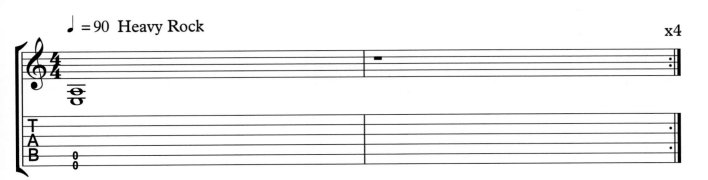

♩ = 90 Heavy Rock

x4

The E Power Chord

If we play our open E on string 6 at the same time as our B on fret 2 of string 5, we are playing a **power chord**. The name of this power chord is **E5**.

The distance between any two given notes is called an **interval**. The interval between the E note and the B is known as a **perfect fifth**, hence the name E5. An **X** above a string indicates that this string is not to be played.

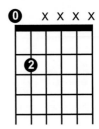

Skatepark

This piece is made up entirely from E5 power chords. The name of the chord is written above the stave. The *f* located underneath the standard notation stands for **forte** and indicates that the piece is to be played loudly. *Forte* is the Italian word for 'loud'. Instructions on how loud or soft a piece of music is to be played are called **dynamics**.

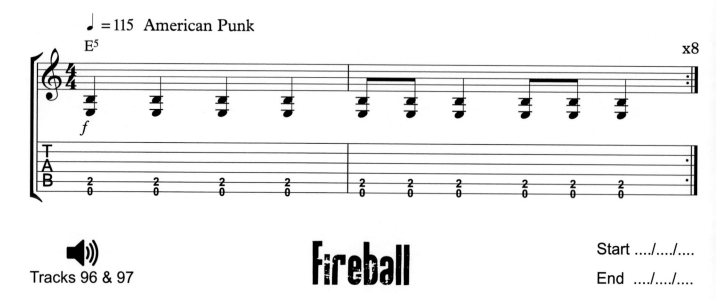

Fireball

This piece uses the E5 power chord as well as single notes. **N.C.** written above the stave indicates that there is **no chord**. Underneath the first note on the standard notation are the letters *mf*. This is another instruction of how loud the piece should be played. In this case, *mf* stands for *mezzo forte* which is the Italian term for 'moderately loud'.

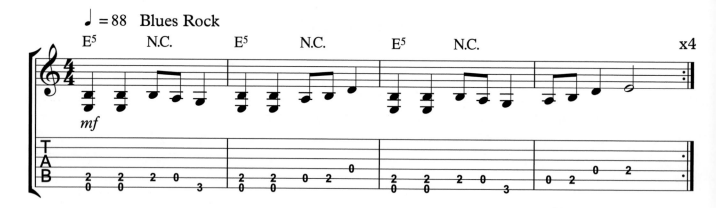

Summary

In this lesson we have learnt how to:

• Understand how to play two notes at once.
• Play the E5 power chord.
• Play pieces with mixed power chords and single lines.
• Understand dynamics.

Things To Remember

• Read the piece of music through fully before you attempt to play it.
• Make sure you read the rhythms correctly and let the notes ring for their full values.
• Read the TAB and standard notation staves when playing your pieces.

More Power Chords

Lesson 17

In this lesson, we are going to look at how we can build power chords on notes other than our E.

The A Power Chord

If we play the open A on string 5 at the same time as the E on fret 2 of our D string, we are playing an A5 power chord.

The E note is a perfect fifth above our A note. The shape of the chord is the same as our E5 but it is on strings 4 and 5.

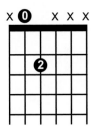

Tracks 98 & 99

Quick Change

Start ..../..../....

End ..../..../....

This piece is an exercise in changing between the A5 and E5 power chords. It is important to give yourself plenty of time to change between chords. Every section is repeated four times and in each one, the number of rests between the chords decreases by one beat. Make sure you change your chord on the beat immediately after you have played the last chord in that bar.

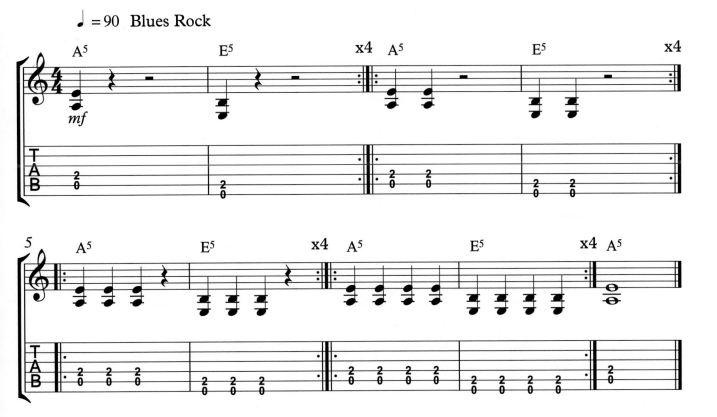

The D Power Chord

The D5 chord is built on our open D string with the A note on string 3 a perfect fifth above it. The chord shape has now moved to strings 3 and 4.

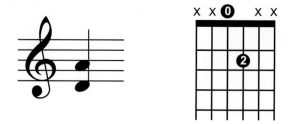

Tracks 100 & 101

The Tor

Start ..../..../....

End ..../..../....

This piece uses our D5, A5 and E5 power chords. If you are finding it difficult to change to the next chord in time, move your finger before the end of the bar in order for the next chord to be in place at the start of the next bar.

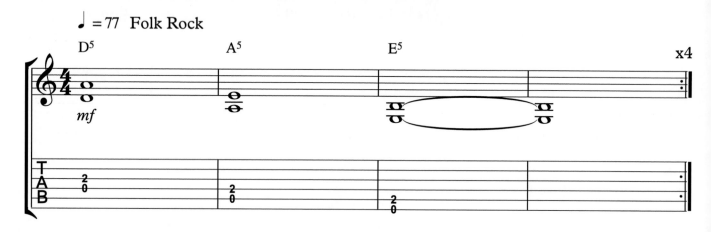

Power Chord Reminder

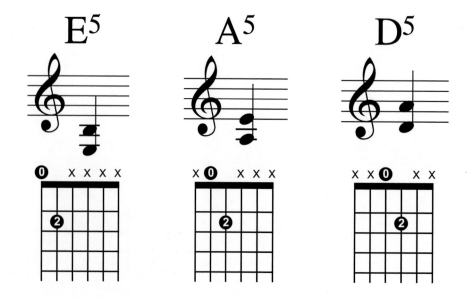

Spooky Soup

Start ..../..../....

End ..../..../....

This piece is made up of A5, D5 and E5 power chords. Listen out for the introduction on the backing track and make sure you pay particular attention to the syncopated rhythm that is played at the beginning of the first line. Bars 1 to 4 are to be played mezzo forte (moderately loud) and bars 5 to 8 are to be played forte (loud). When changing from E5 to D5, it is important that the open E on string 6 doesn't ring over the D5 chord.

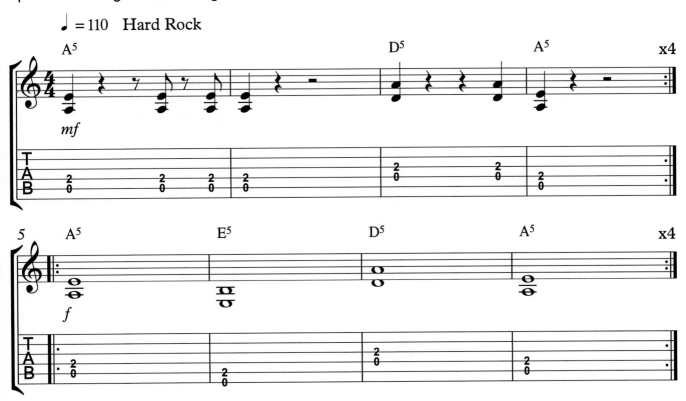

Les Paul
1915-2009

Profile As well as being an accomplished guitarist, Les Paul was also a renowned guitar luthier and innovator of studio recording techniques. Throughout the 1950s Les Paul performed and recorded with his wife Mary Ford and together they went on to sell millions of records. He was also one of the pioneers of the solid body electric guitar and in 1952, Gibson began to manufacture the Les Paul guitar which subsequently became one of the defining instruments in Rock and Pop music history.

Playlist - How High The Moon, Viya Con Dios, Whither Thou Goest

Summary

In this lesson we have learnt how to:

• Play A5 and D5 power chords.
• Play pieces of music with mixed A5, D5 and E5 power chords.
• Practise changing between power chords.

Things To Remember

• Use the exercise in Quick Change to help you shift between power chords.
• Give yourself plenty of time when changing between chords.
• Play along with the backing tracks.

More Syncopation

This is a commonly used syncopated rhythm. It is made up of a quaver, a crotchet and a quaver.

1   &   (2)   &

We can look at this rhythm as four quavers with the second and third tied together.

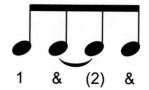

1   &   (2)   &

Tracks 104 & 105

Satchel

Start ..../..../....

End ..../..../....

This piece uses the syncopated rhythm from above and combines power chords with single notes. Watch out for the accented note at the beginning of bar 4. Remember, we play an accented note with slightly more force than the rest of the notes in the piece.

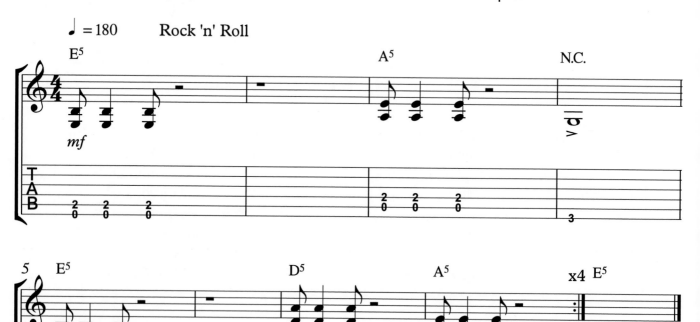

One Drop

This piece uses the syncopated rhythm from the beginning of this lesson in bars 3 and 7.

Roswell

This piece uses consecutive occurrences of the syncopated rhythm. Listen out for the rhythm at the end of bar 8.

Summary

In this lesson we have learnt how to:

• Play more complex syncopated rhythms.
• Play more pieces of music with mixed A5, D5 and E5 power chords.

Things To Remember

• Be aware of the pulse when playing syncopated rhythms.
• Try not to look at your hands when playing
• Hold your plectrum correctly and rest your picking hand on your bridge.

Sharps

In order to understand what a sharp is, we are going to use the notes that we have learnt on string 1. In between the F on fret 1 and the G on fret 3, we have a new note called F sharp (F♯). We play this note with finger 2. F♯ can always be found one fret higher than F. Sharpening a note raises its pitch by one fret. The distance of one fret is also known as a **semitone**.

Tracks 110 & 111

Comanche

Start ..../..../....

End ..../..../....

All the F notes in this piece are sharpened. Listen out for the introduction on the backing track and remember to observe the fermata in the final bar.

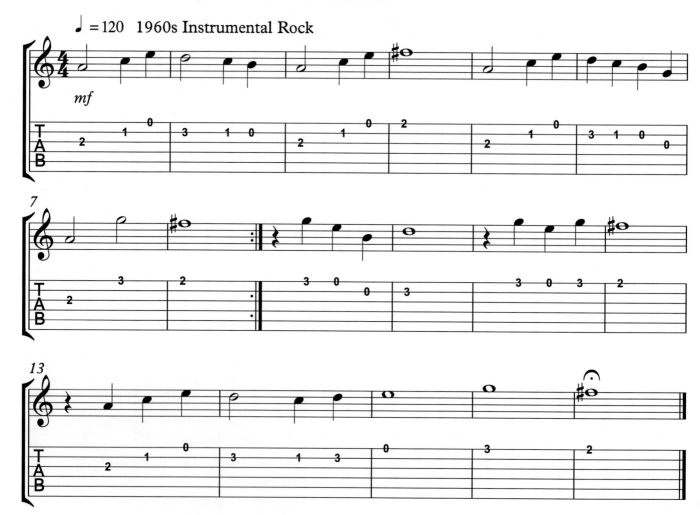

The G Major Scale

All the notes in the previous piece belong to the G major scale. The G major scale contains the same notes as the G major pentatonic scale with the addition of the C note on fret 1 of string 2 and the new F♯ on fret 2 of string 1.

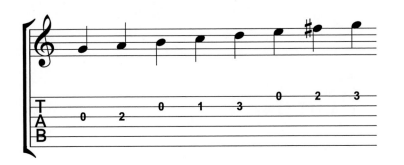
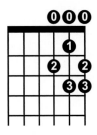

D String F Sharp

This F♯ note is found on **fret 4** of our **fourth string**. We play this note with the **fourth finger** of our fretting hand.

It is a good idea to get used to using finger 4 to play this note, even if it is tempting to play it with a different finger.

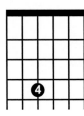

Tracks 112 & 113

Billy The Kid

Start ..../..../....

End ..../..../....

In this piece, we use the F♯ on string 4. Remember to use finger 4 on your fretting hand to play this note.

55

Low F Sharp

Just like the low F, the low F# is written on the **third ledger line** underneath the stave. The stem of the low F# note points **upwards**.

This F# note is found on **fret 2** of our **sixth string**. We play this note with the **second finger** of our fretting hand.

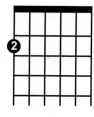

Tracks 114 & 115

Nebraska

Start ..../..../....

End ..../..../....

In this piece, we use the low F# note. Make sure you let the notes ring for their full values.

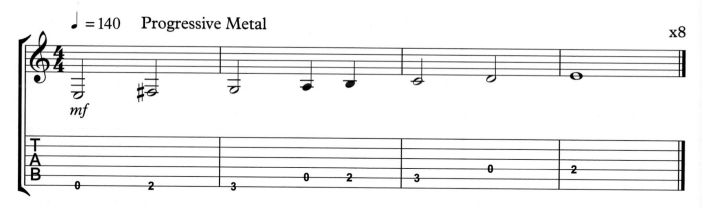

We can use the notes we have just learnt to create two new two octave scales. The G major scale and the E natural minor scale contain the same notes and just as we discovered in Lesson 14, the tonality depends on which note we use as the root note.

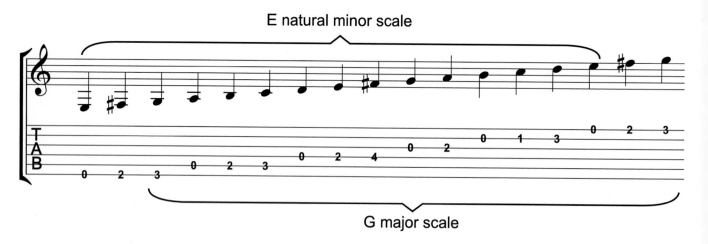

Summary

In this lesson we have learnt how to:

- Identify and play F# notes on strings 1, 4 and 6.
- Play two octave G major and E natural minor scales
- Use finger 4 on our fretting hand.

Things To Remember

- Press down the notes with the tips of your fretting hand fingers.
- Read the rhythms correctly and let the notes ring for their full values.
- F# notes can always be found one fret higher than F notes.

The Blue Note

In Lesson 19 we learnt about sharpened notes. Remember, to sharpen a note, we raise its pitch by a semitone. Similarly, if we lower a note by a semitone, we call this a **flattened note**. The symbol for a flat looks like this ♭. We can use a flattened note to add more colour to our E minor pentatonic scale. In the key of E minor, this note is the B♭ and is referred to as the **blue note**.

🔊
Tracks 116 & 117

The Cross

Start ..../..../....
End ..../..../....

The blue note can be found in bars 2 and 4 and gives the whole piece an eerie sound. The name that we give to a flattened or sharpened note is an **accidental**. An accidental lasts for the duration of the bar that it occurs in and is cancelled out by a **bar line** or a **natural sign** which looks like this ♮.

♩ = 90 Heavy Metal

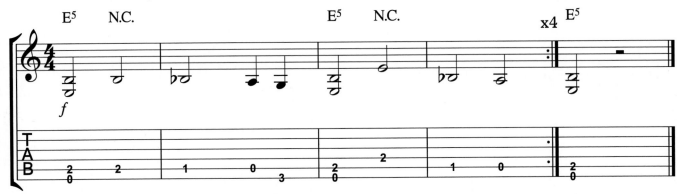

🔊
Tracks 118 & 119

Night Watchman

Start ..../..../....
End ..../..../....

The dynamic marking *mf* indicates that we are to play the first line **mezzo forte** which means **moderately loud**. The rest of the piece is to be played **forte**.

♩ = 150 Alternative Rock

57

With the addition of this blue note, we have a new scale called the **blues scale.** Below is a descending form of the E blues scale. Remember, it is a good idea to practise the scale both ascending and descending.

Tracks 120 & 121

Nine Lives

Start ..../..../....

End ..../..../....

The E blues scale can be found in this piece in bars 2 and 6. The dynamic marking is $f\!f$. This stands for **fortissimo** which means **very loud.**

♩ = 90   Hard Rock

Summary

In this lesson we have learnt how to:

- Identify and play the B♭ note on string 5.
- Play a one octave E blues scale.
- Understand the dynamic marking $f\!f$.

Things To Remember

- Use the correct fretting hand fingers.
- Read both staves.
- Don't look at your hands when playing the pieces.

Moveable Power Chords

We have already looked at power chords and how we can move them onto different strings. In this lesson, we are going to focus on how to move power chords onto different frets. **Moveable power chords** are very versatile and enable us to create more interesting **riffs** and **chord progressions**.

If we look at the **E5** power chord that we learnt in Lesson 16, we can see that it is made up of our **open E** on string 6 and our **B** on fret 2 of string 5. Remember that we call this interval a **perfect fifth**.

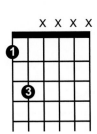

If we move both our open E a **semitone higher** to the **F** on fret 1 of string 6 and our B to the **C** on fret 3 of string 5, we still have an interval of a perfect fifth, but both pitches have changed. We now have a power chord with an F as its root note. It has become an **F5**. We play this new chord with fingers 1 and 3 of our fretting hand.

Tracks 122 & 123

Jack Frost

Start ..../..../....

End ..../..../....

This piece uses the F5 power chord. It is important to use the correct fretting hand thumb position as indicated in Lesson 10. From bars 5 to 9, try leaving finger 3 on the C note on fret 3 of string 5. This will make the transition between the F5 and the open E note a little smoother.

The G Power Chord

We learnt in Lesson 10 that the note on fret 3 of string 6 is a G. We can build a power chord on this note. The interval is still a perfect fifth and because we are using a G as our root note, we are playing a **G5 power chord**.

In this diagram, the direction **3 fr** indicates that this power chord is to be played at fret 3. The same fingers that we used for our F5 power chord are used. In this instance, the F on string 6 fret 1 has moved two frets to a G at fret 3 and the C on string 5 fret 3 has moved two frets to a D.

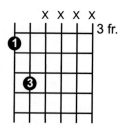

Tracks 124 & 125

Water Slide

Start ..../..../....
End ..../..../....

This piece uses our G5 and F5 power chords. Use the rest in bars 4 and 6 to change chords. When changing between the G5 and F5 power chords, try to move your hand to the next chord without changing the position of your fingers. Both chords use the same fingers so all you have to do is relax your thumb to move your hand. For an extra challenge, try not to look at your hands when changing chords.

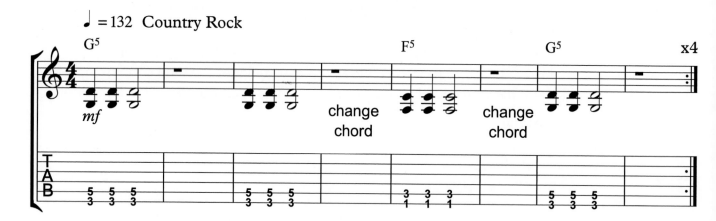

It is important to note that the D note that you are playing on string 5 as part of your G5 power chord is in actual fact the same as the open D note on string 4 that we learnt in Lesson 13. The majority of notes on the guitar can be played in more than one position. Play both D notes and listen to how they are the same pitch.

60

Donut

We use a mixture of moveable power chords (G5 and F5) and open power chords (E5, A5 and D5) in this piece. We are also introduced to a new symbol in bars 2 and 14. This symbol is a **single bar repeat sign** and simply indicates that you should play the same as the previous bar. Pay particular attention to the change in dynamics at bar 5 and again at bar 13. It is also important to practise the change between the F5 and G5 at bars 3 to 4 and also 15 to 16.

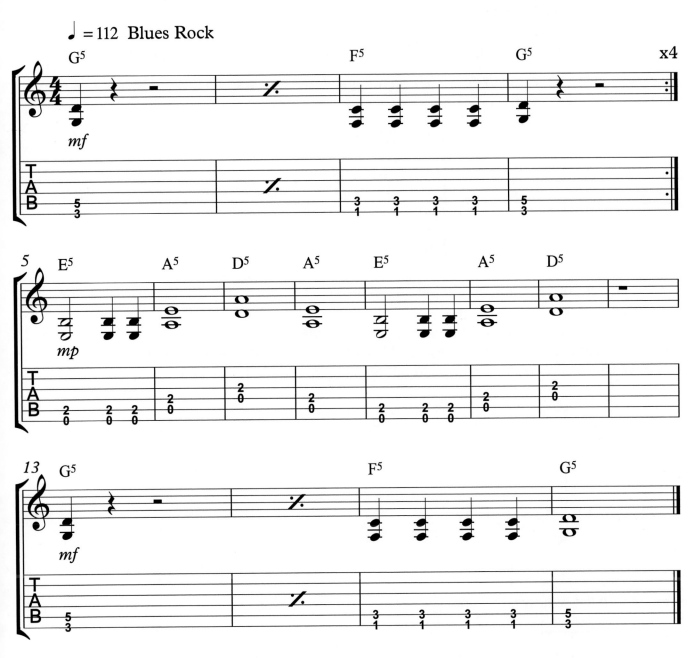

Summary

In this lesson we have learnt how to:

• Play a sixth string root moveable power chord shape.
• Play pieces using mixed fretted and open power chords.

Things To Remember

• Use the correct fretting hand thumb position when playing moveable power chord shapes.
• Give yourself plenty of time when changing between chords.
• Try not to look at your hands when changing between chords.

Mapping Out String Six

The sixth string root power chord can be played anywhere on string 6. In order to play power chords further up the neck of the guitar, it is essential that we learn the way that the notes are set out. We learnt in Lesson 9 that the musical alphabet runs in a continuous sequence from A through to G and then begins again, like this:

A B C D E F G A B C D E F G etc.

This sequence can be found anywhere on the guitar and can start on any letter. For instance, we have already learnt the notes below on string 6:

In order to get from one note to another in the musical alphabet, we have to move either one fret (a semitone) or two frets (a tone). The distance between E and F is always a semitone and F to G is always a tone. Tones occur between all of the notes in the sequence, except for E to F and B to C. In both these instances, the interval is that of a semitone. If we were to look at one octave of the musical alphabet mapped out on string 6 it would look like this:

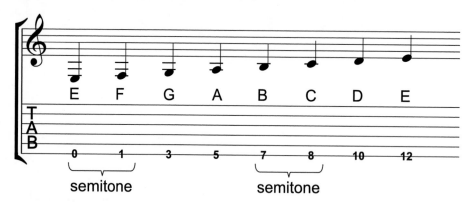

After fret 12, the sequence begins again, only this time an octave higher. It is a good idea to try to memorise this pattern and the names of each note both ascending and descending.

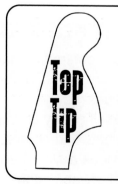

Many guitars have dots on their neck. These are called **fret markers** or **inlays** and are there to help us navigate the frets of the guitar. These dots are usually found at frets 3, 5, 7, 9 and a double dot at fret 12 (the octave). The pattern then repeats beyond fret 12. Try to use these dots to help you find your way around string 6.

The sixth string root power chord shape can be played with its root note on any of the notes on string 6. For instance, if we wanted to play a power chord with its root on a B on string 6, we would first locate the B at fret 7 and then build the chord on that note.

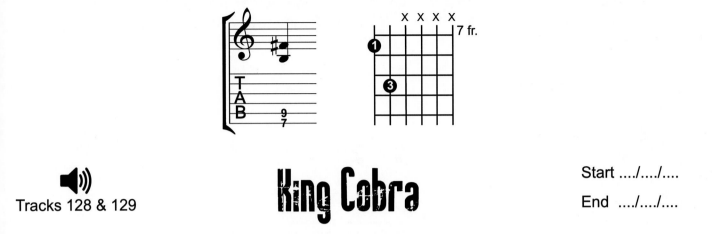

Tracks 128 & 129

King Cobra

Start ..../..../....

End ..../..../....

In this piece, we use three power chords. G5 is at fret 3, A5 is at fret 5 and B5 is at fret 7. You can use your fret markers to help you find each of these chords. Listen out for the introduction played on guitar and remember to repeat the first four bars five times.

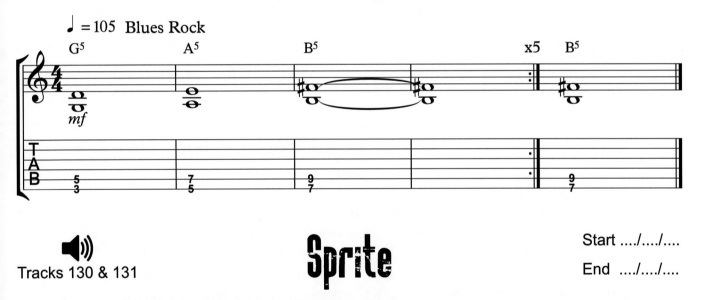

Tracks 130 & 131

Sprite

Start ..../..../....

End ..../..../....

This piece makes use of G5 at fret 3, B5 at fret 7 and C5 at fret 8. Remember to keep your fretting hand shape when moving between the chords.

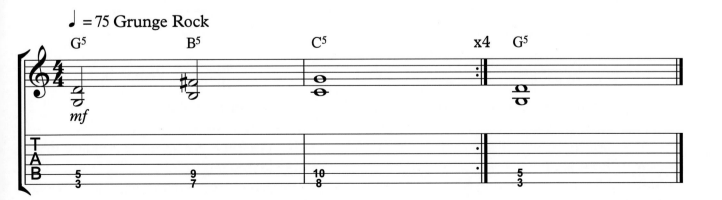

Top Hat

In this piece, we use a mixture of power chords and single notes. It is a good idea to use your first finger for the last two notes in bar 4. Watch out for the rhythm and make sure you repeat the first eight bars.

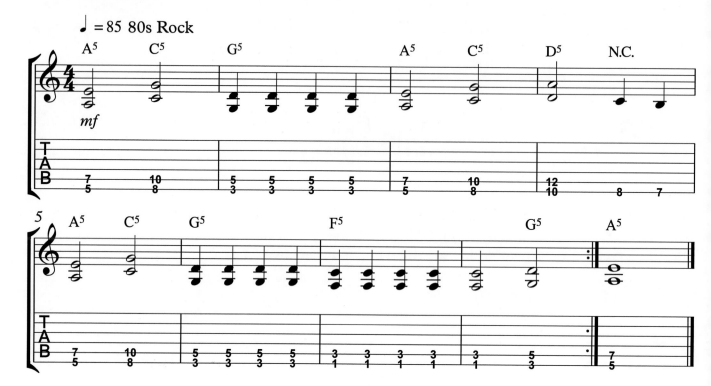

Slash
b1965

Summary

In this lesson we have learnt how to:

• Play a moveable sixth string root power chord shape.
• Map out the notes on string 6.
• Move our power chord shape up and down the neck.

Things To Remember

• Try to memorise the position of the notes on string 6.
• Use the fret markers on your guitar to help locate the frets.
• Make sure your fretting hand thumb is in the correct position.

Lesson 23

Fifth String Root

In the previous lesson, we looked at how the notes are set out on string 6. The notes on string 5 follow exactly the same pattern, only this time our starting point is an A note. Remember, the semitone intervals occur between the notes B and C and also E and F.

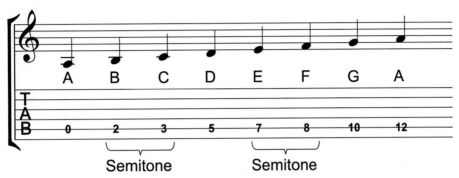

We are now able to play moveable power chords using our fifth string as a root note.

Tracks 134 & 135

Toronto

Start ..../..../....

End ..../..../....

This piece uses E5, D5, B5 and C5 power chords. Give yourself plenty of time and try to change chords as soon as possible during the rests. Just like in The Bomb from Lesson 7, this piece begins with a crotchet rest.

♩ = 140 80s Rock

Spelling Test

In this piece, we use a mixture of fifth string and sixth string root power chords. Watch out for the repeat in bar 2 and the *D.C.* at the end of bar 4. On the recording, the backing track starts with a rhythm guitar introduction before the bass guitar and drums begin. The guitar part starts after the snare drum fill.

Duration Reminder

Below is a list of the note values and their corresponding rests that we have covered in this book. Remember, the value of the notes are all relative to the crotchet taking one beat.

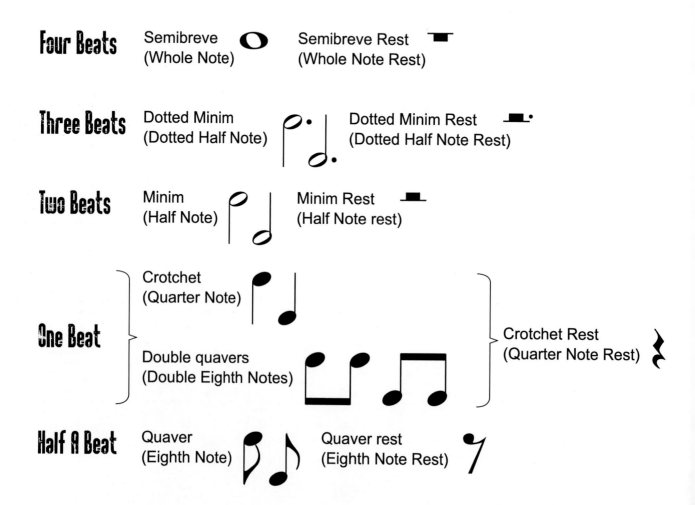

Spectrum

This piece uses root 6 and root 5 power chords as well as single notes. We can also see the direction **D.C. al Coda** in bar 20. Remember, **D.C.** stands for **Da Capo** which means 'back to the beginning' and then when indicated, (**To Coda**) we go to the **Coda** which looks like this ⊕. Coda is the Italian word for 'tail' and is usually found at the end of a piece of music.

Summary

In this lesson we have learnt how to:

- Map out and play power chords on string 5.
- Play pieces with mixed fifth and sixth string root power chords.
- Identify and understand **D.C. al coda**.

Things To Remember

- Try to memorise the position of the notes on string 5.
- Use the fret markers on your guitar to help locate the frets.
- Semitones occur between B to C and E to F.

Moveable Scale Shapes

We now know how to move power chords up and down the neck of the guitar. The same principle can be applied to our minor pentatonic scale. Let's take another look at the E minor pentatonic shape that we learnt in Lesson 14.

We can move this shape up and down the fretboard in exactly the same way as we did with our power chords. If we move the E minor pentatonic scale one fret higher, we have an **F minor pentatonic scale**. All the notes have been raised by one fret but it is still the same scale shape. It is important to note that we play this version of the minor pentatonic scale with different fingers to the E minor pentatonic above.

Let's transpose the shape up to the fifth fret and play a one octave **A minor pentatonic scale**. We are now playing this scale in **fifth position**.

Steady Rock

The A minor pentatonic shape from the previous page is used throughout this piece. Make sure you use the correct fretting hand fingers.

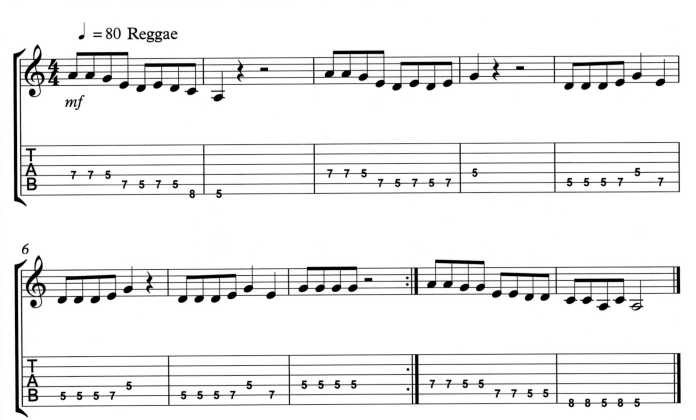

We can also add the notes from the upper octave of this scale to make a **two octave A minor pentatonic scale**.

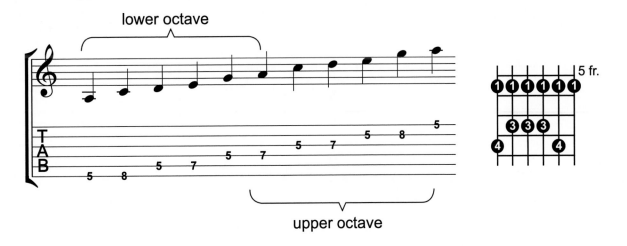

Duck Walk

In this piece, we play a lot of **double-stopped** notes using the notes on fret 5 of both the first and second strings. Instead of using two separate fingers, we can use just our first finger. This is more economical and is a useful technique when playing two separate notes at the same fret on adjacent strings. In order to execute this technique, we have to use the pad of our first finger rather than the tip. This is called a **half barre**.

This piece is to be played three times as indicated on the music. During the second playing, as we did with The Bomb, we will play an improvised solo. On the third time through, play the piece as written. In this piece, we will use four notes from our two octave minor pentatonic scale to improvise with. Remember, so long as you use the correct notes, you can play whatever you like and it will sound right.

70

Marquee

This time, we have moved our root note up to fret 7 on string 6. We are now playing the B minor pentatonic scale. The rhythm found in bars 1, 3, 13 and 15 is the same syncopated rhythm we learnt in Lesson 18.

♩ = 115 Memphis Soul

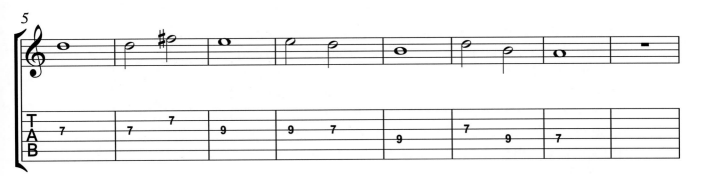

Summary

In this lesson we have learnt how to:

• Play a two octave moveable minor pentatonic shape.
• Play double-stopped notes using a half barre.
• Improvise using four notes from the moveable minor pentatonic shape.

Things To Remember

• Remember to use the correct fingers when playing the moveable minor pentatonic scale shape.
• Make sure you can hear both notes when playing the half barre on strings 1 and 2.
• Rest your picking hand on the bridge to help you to find the correct strings.

Open Chords

Although we have learnt how to play power chords, technically these are not chords as they only contain two notes. The correct term for a chord that contains only two notes (such as a power chord) is a **dyad**. In order for a chord to be classed as such, it must contain three or more notes. The two most common types of chords are **major** and **minor** and are both forms of **triads**.

The Open E Minor Chord

If we finger a B note on fret 2 of string 5 at the same time as fingering an E on fret 2 of string 4 then strum all six strings, we are playing an **open E minor chord**. This chord is classed as an open chord. Open chords are chords that contain one or more open strings.

If we play the chord from string 6, our open E minor chord (or **Em**) contains the notes **E, B, E, G, B and E**. Playing the notes E, B and G in any combination gives us an **Em chord**. It is important that you use the tips of your fingers to press down the chord shape to ensure that all of the notes in the chord are ringing without any dead or buzzing notes. You can check this by playing each note of the chord individually.

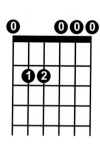

🔊
Tracks 146 & 147

Knife Hand Strike

Start ..../..../....

End ..../..../....

Unlike individual string picking, your strumming hand is not required to rest on the bridge of the guitar. Strum all of the strings in a downward motion and be careful to strum from your wrist rather than from your elbow. Stop the chord in the second bar by resting the side of your strumming hand on all of your strings. The chord symbol for the Em is written above the stave.

♩ = 80   Indie Rock

Chord Changes

This next piece is an exercise in how to change between two different chords. Our first chord is **Em**.

If we move our second finger to our G on string 6 fret 3, we have changed to a new chord. The name of this chord is **G6**.

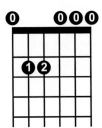
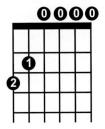

Transformers

Tracks 148 & 149

Start ..../..../....

End ..../..../....

In order to make sure that the chord changes are smooth, give yourself plenty of time when moving your fingers between each chord. Each section of the piece is played four times.

♩=70 Folk Rock

La Habana

The Open G Chord

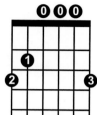

This piece introduces us to the **open G major chord** (or **G**). When we change from Em to G, we keep the first finger on the B located on string 5. The second finger moves to the G on string 6 and we add the high G on string 1 with our third finger.

Summary

In this lesson we have learnt how to:

• Play our open Em, G6 and G chords.
• Change between our Em, G and G6 chords.
• Play pieces of music with chord window diagrams.

Things To Remember

• Make sure all your notes from your chords sound clean.
• Strum towards the floor from your wrist.
• Give yourself plenty of time when changing chords.

Slurred Notes

The Hammer-On

Slurred notes are executed by picking the string once and then using our fretting hand to create more notes. There are several ways to play slurred notes. The first one that we will look at is the **hammer-on**. We will start by playing our open G on string 3. We then 'hammer' the second finger of our fretting hand onto the A on fret 2. Make sure you use the tip of your finger and place it as close to the fret wire as possible. The movement of your finger onto the fretted note has to be done with enough force to make the hammered note sound whilst still ensuring the notes last for their correct values.

Although the curved line joining the two notes resembles the symbol for a tied note, the pitches of the two notes in this example are different so the music indicates that this is to be played as a slur. The letter **H** underneath the TAB stave tells us that it is a hammer-on.

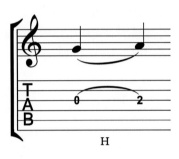

Tracks 152 & 153

Slinky

Start ..../..../....

End ..../..../....

This piece is simply an exercise in hammering-on from your open G on string 3 to your A on fret 2. Listen out for the introduction and remember to let the notes ring for their full values.

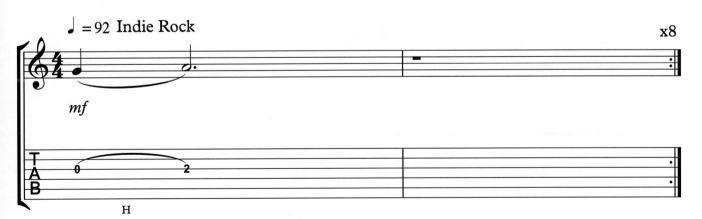

The Pull-Off

The second type of slur we will look at is called a **pull-off**. This time, we will start by playing the A note on fret 2 of string 3 with the second finger on our fretting hand. We then use the fretting hand finger to pluck the string towards the floor to produce an open G note. A letter **P** is written under the stave to indicate a pull-off.

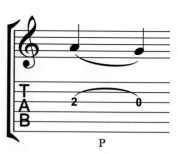

Tracks 154 & 155

See More

Start ..../..../....

End ..../..../....

This piece uses the pull-off technique as highlighted above. It is important to differentiate between the curved line symbol for the pull-off between the first two notes and the tied note. Remember, the slurred notes are different pitches connected by a curved line whereas the tied notes are of the same pitch.

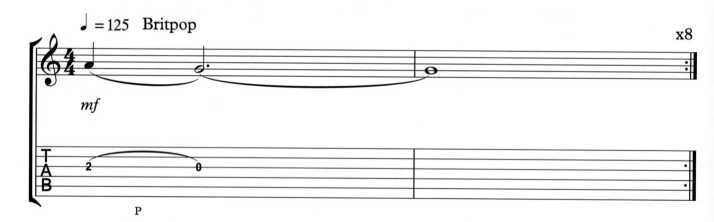

Johnny Marr
b1963

Johnny Marr's distinctive style has influenced countless guitarists and helped to define Indie Rock as a genre. During the 80s when most guitar heroes favoured distorted riffs and virtuosic solos, Marr's guitar playing with The Smiths used clean tones with shimmering chorus effects, clever use of open strings and altered tunings. Since The Smiths disbanded in 1987, Marr has gone on to work with several other acts and also as a solo artist.

Playlist - This Charming Man, How Soon is Now, Panic

Boardwalk

This piece uses hammer-ons and pull-offs. Listen out for the introduction on the backing track and make sure all the notes ring for their full values.

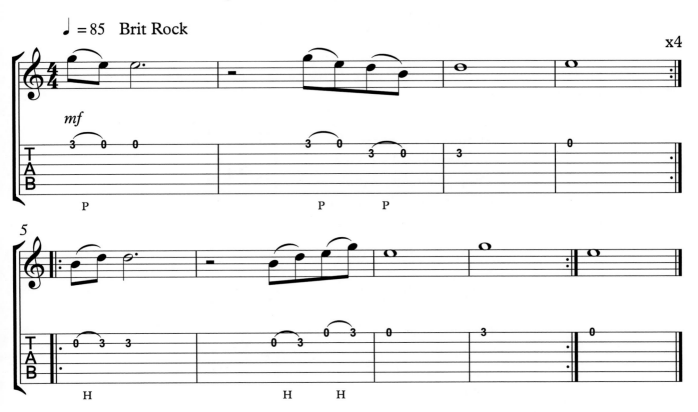

A good technique for practising hammer-ons is to not play the note you are hammering-on from. If you can manage to make the second note sound without playing the first of the two notes, you know that you are executing the slur with enough force. Likewise, if you can make the second note of a pull-off sound without picking the first note, you can be sure you are managing to pluck the string correctly with your fretting hand.

Summary

In this lesson we have learnt how to:

- Hammer-on from an open string.
- Pull-off to an open string
- Play combinations of hammer-ons and pull-offs.

Things To Remember

- Use your fingertip to fret notes.
- Make sure you let notes ring for their full values.
- When executing a pull-off, pluck the note with your fretting hand.

More Open Chords

The Am and C Open Chords

In this lesson, we are going to learn how to play more open chords. The next two new open chords are **A minor** (**Am**) and **C**.

This is our **open Am chord**. Remember, the symbol x (in this case on string 6) indicates that we don't play this string when strumming the chord.

This is our **open C chord**. When changing from our Am to our C chord, all we need to do is move our third finger from the A note on fret 2 of string 3 to the C on fret 3 of string 5. All the other fingers stay the same.

🔊

Tracks 158 & 159

Postcard

Start ..../..../....

End ..../..../....

This piece uses Am and C chords. Remember to change chords during the rests. For an extra challenge, try to improvise different rhythms when strumming.

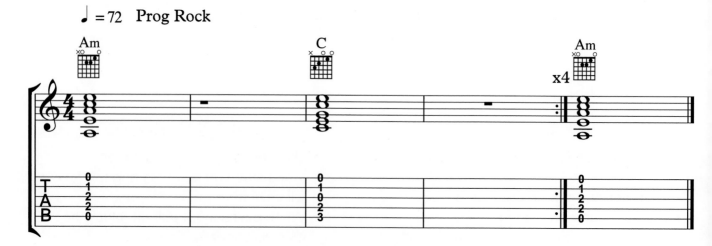

The Open D Chord

This is our **open D chord**. We only strum our first four strings on this chord. Make sure you use the correct fingers.

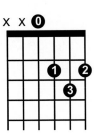

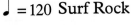

Tracks 160 & 161

Shotgun Rider

Start ..../..../....

End ..../..../....

This piece uses the Em and D chords. Again, like in Postcard, for an extra challenge, try to vary the strumming and improvise your own rhythms to make it sound interesting.

♩ = 120 Surf Rock

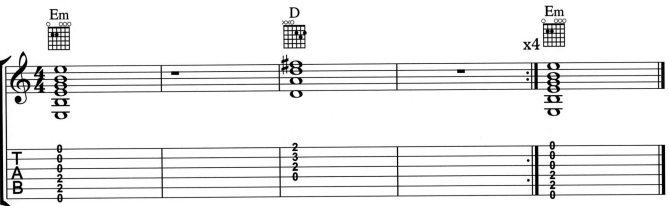

Frank Zappa
1940-1993

Although Frank Zappa was principally a self-taught musician, his body of work spanned musical genres including Rock 'n' Roll, Jazz, Avant-Garde and Orchestral pieces. During a 30 year career, Zappa released over 60 albums which included many guitar solos that showcased his unique improvisational style. Zappa continues to be considered one of the most visionary and innovative musicians of his generation.

Playlist - Peaches en Regalia, Watermelon in Easter Hay, Zoot Allures

Legend

This piece uses the chord sequence **G**, **D**, **Em** and **C**. This is a very common chord sequence that can be found in many songs. Remember to try to vary the strumming by improvising your own rhythms.

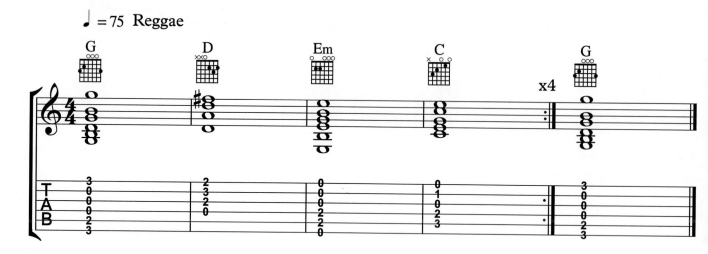

Bob Marley
1945-1981

Robert Nesta Marley was born in Jamaica and with his group The Wailers and also as a solo artist was one of the pioneers of Reggae music. His main guitar was a 1970s Gibson Les Paul Special which can now be found in the Bob Marley Museum in Kingston, Jamaica. The 1984 greatest hits album Legend has sold an estimated 28 million copies worldwide and is the best selling Reggae album of all time.

Playlist - No Woman No Cry, Get Up, Stand Up, Is This Love

Summary

In this lesson we have learnt how to:

- Play our Am, C and D Chords.
- Change between our Am, C, Em, D and G chords.
- Improvise strumming patterns.

Things To Remember

- Use the tips of your fingers when playing your chords.
- Give yourself plenty of time when changing between chords.
- Make sure you are strumming the correct strings.

Arpeggios

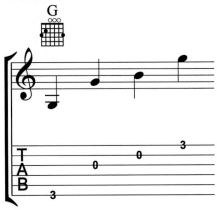

As well as strumming chords, we can also use them to play **arpeggios**. When executing an arpeggio (sometimes called a **broken chord**) we play notes taken from a chord in succession instead of simultaneously. For example, we could play an arpeggio by fretting a G chord and then playing strings 6, 3, 2 and 1 in succession. Make sure you hold the chord down throughout and let the notes ring.

Dal Segno

Dal Segno is an instruction in music notation that tells us to repeat a passage of music. It is Italian for "from the sign" and is often abbreviated to just *D.S.* It works in much the same way as *Da Capo* but instead of going back and repeating the whole piece, we can specify a particular bar to repeat from. We use the sign 𝄋 to indicate where the piece of music is to be repeated from.

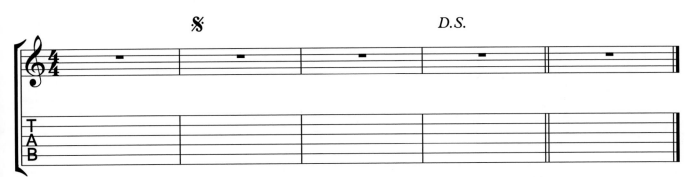

In the above example, we would play the music up to bar 4 where the *D.S.* tells us to repeat from the 𝄋 at bar 2.

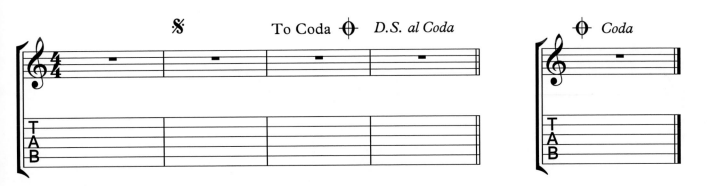

This example uses the symbol 𝄋 and a *Coda*. The piece tells us to play up to bar 4 where we repeat from bar 2 and then go to the *Coda* after playing bar 3.

Sunshine

In this piece we use arpeggiated versions of Em, C, G, D and Am chords. Make sure the notes are left to ring out as indicated on the score. Watch out for the repeats and the *D.S. al Coda* direction at bar 12. The wavy line in the final bar tells us that the Em chord is to be strummed. It's a good idea to practise the chord changes prior to attempting the arpeggios. You could do this by strumming the chords on the first beat of each bar to get your fretting hand used to the chords.

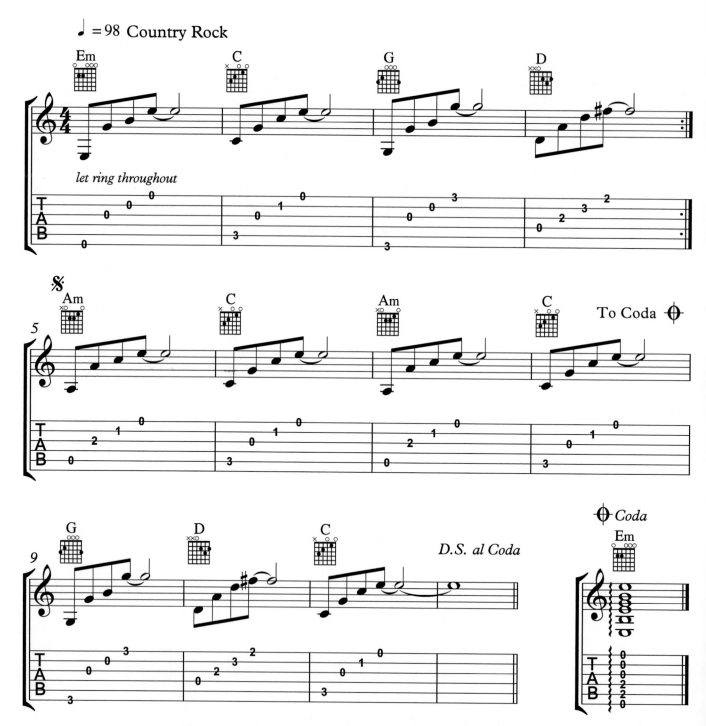

U.F.O.

This piece uses our D, Am, C and Em chords. Remember to use the chord change exercise before attempting this piece. If you hear any dead or buzzing notes, remember to check that you are playing the chords with the tips of your fretting hand fingers and that they aren't touching any other strings.

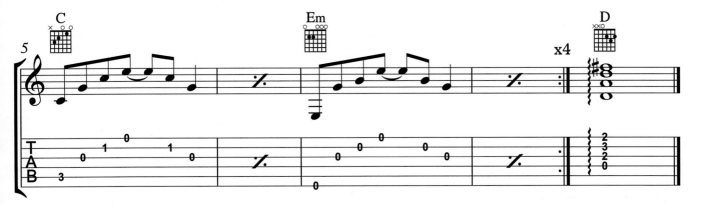

Different Time Signatures

Up to now, all the pieces that we have learnt have used the $\frac{4}{4}$ time signature. We are now going to learn a piece that is written using a different time signature. The new time signature we are going to learn has **two crotchet beats** in a bar instead of four.

Two ——— $\mathbf{2}$

Crotchets ——— $\mathbf{\frac{}{4}}$
(Quarter notes)

Remember, when looking at a time signature, the top number tells us how many beats are in a bar, and the bottom number tells us what type of note is worth one beat of the pulse.

Rickjangles

This piece has **two crotchet beats** in a bar and combines single notes, arpeggiated chords and strummed chords. In order to distinguish between single notes and either a strummed or arpeggiated chord being played, we use the letters **N.C.** (which stand for **no chord**) or the relevant chord symbol. Make sure the arpeggiated notes ring out where marked and the chords are strummed when indicated. Remember, a sharp lasts for the duration of the bar that it occurs in so the third note in bar 2 is also an F♯. It is also important to note that the F♯ at the end of bar 3 carries over to the first note in bar 4 that it is tied to and therefore doesn't require a sharp. The first note that we play is a **dotted crotchet** which lasts for **one and a half beats**.

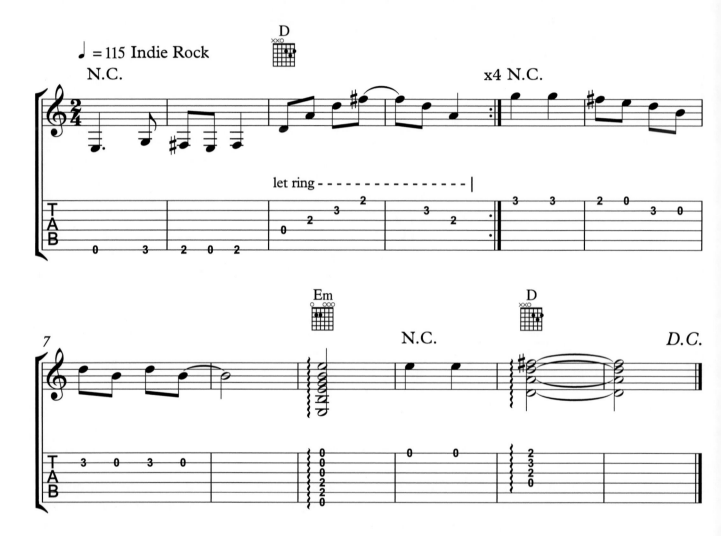

Summary

In this lesson we have learnt how to:

- Identify and play arpeggiated chords.
- Understand and play pieces with a *Dal Segno* direction.
- Understand and play pieces using a $\frac{2}{4}$ time signature

Things To Remember

- Make sure that you are fretting your chords correctly.
- Let the notes of each arpeggiated chord ring out.
- Try not to look at either of your hands.

Lesson 29

Three in A Bar

In this lesson we are going to look at pieces of music with three crotchet beats in each bar. Remember, a time signature can be viewed as a fraction. In this case, the fraction would be three quarters (three crotchets).

Three — $\dfrac{3}{4}$
Crotchets —
(Quarter notes)

The Open A Chord

This is our **open A chord**. The A chord uses 5 strings so be careful not to play string 6 (your low E). It is also important that you make sure your third finger doesn't touch the first string otherwise string 1 (your high E) won't ring.

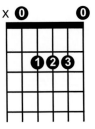

🔊 Tracks 170 & 171

Let's Have it!

Start ..../..../....
End ..../..../....

This piece introduces the $\dfrac{3}{4}$ time signature as well as the A major chord. Make sure you count each dotted minim carefully and watch out for the repeat at the end of bar 8.

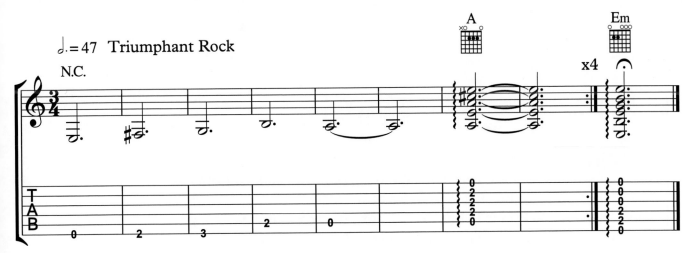

85

Scandinavia

Start ..../..../....
End ..../..../....

This piece uses the ***D.C. al Coda*** direction. It's also important to note that the tempo marking refers to the dotted minim and not the crotchet as we have seen previously.

♩.=50 Psychedelic Rock

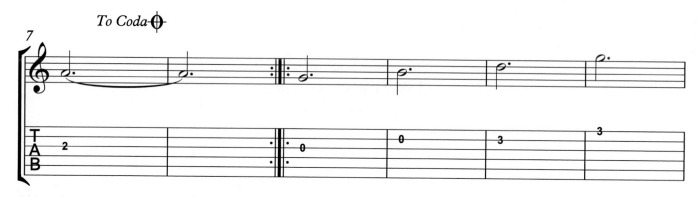

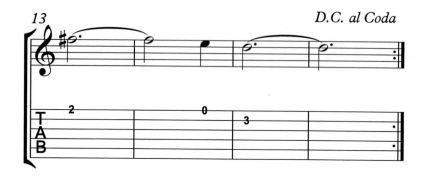

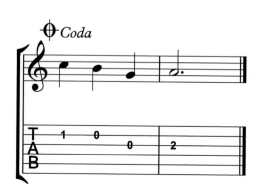

George Harrison
1943-2001

Profile Known as "the quiet Beatle", George Harrison's work with the Fab Four and subsequent solo career demonstrated an eclectic mix of influences from Rock 'n' Roll to Indian music that continues to inspire generations of musicians to this day. His use of slide guitar and 12 string Rickenbacker playing as well as catchy riffs and melodic soloing gave The Beatles' sound a distinctive edge that made them arguably the most influential band in popular music history.

Playlist - Here Comes The Sun, While My Guitar Gently Weeps, My Sweet Lord

Materialise

Start ..../..../....

End ..../..../....

It is important to make sure the notes last for their full values when playing this piece. Get your fingers ready for the shift up to fifth position in preparation for the D5 power chord at bar 17.

♩.= 43 Progressive Rock

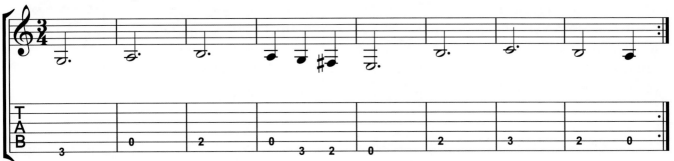

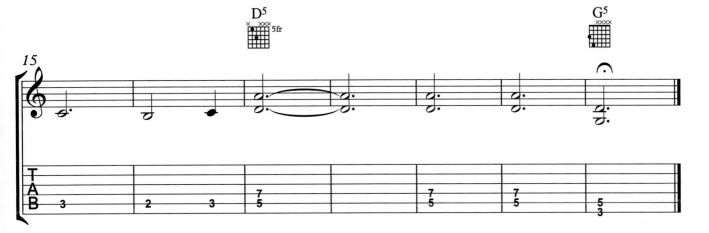

Summary

In this lesson we have learnt how to:

• Identify and play pieces with a $\frac{3}{4}$ time signature.
• Play the open A major chord.
• Understand how to use different note values when indicating the tempo.

Things To Remember

• Make sure that you count each bar correctly.
• Listen to the backing tracks and feel the pulse.
• Listen for buzzing notes and press down the string behind the fret using the tip of your finger.

Lesson 30

Strumming Patterns

Two New Chords

This is our open **E major chord**. it looks very similar to the Am chord that we learnt in Lesson 27. Our open E uses all six strings.

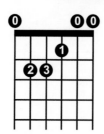

This is our **open B7 chord**. We need to get used to using all four fretting hand fingers when playing this chord.

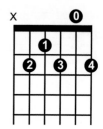

The next piece requires us to change between the E and B7 chords. When executing any chord change, try to move your fingers as little as possible. When changing between these two chords, you can keep your second finger on the B note on string 5. The first and third fingers swap strings and then the fourth finger is added onto the F# on fret 2 of the first string. Make sure you practise this change using the exercise from Lesson 25.

Up-Strums

Up to now, all the strums we have used have been down-strums. That is to say, our picking hand has always strummed the strings in a downward motion towards the floor. In order to make our rhythms more interesting, we can add up-strums to our strumming patterns. Let's start by adding a single up-strum in a simple four-beat pattern between the third and fourth beat.

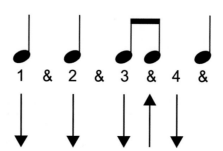

In order to play the strumming pattern in time with the pulse, make sure your hand is moving in a constant down/up motion throughout. It is important to note that your hand is still moving in an upwards direction between all the beats, however, the only time that your plectrum actually strikes the strings off the beat is between the third and fourth beat. When performing this strum, don't attempt to play all the strings, just aim for two or three strings to make it sound smooth and relaxed.

Top Tip

You can practise strumming without the need for your guitar. Try strumming against your leg or your other hand when your instrument isn't available.

Motel

In this piece, we use the strumming pattern we have just learnt as well as the E, A and B7 chords. In this piece, we use a **double bar repeat sign** in bars 3 and 4. This tells us to play the same as the previous two bars. Remember to give yourself plenty of time when changing between chords. The piece begins with a one bar rest.

♩=109   Blues Rock

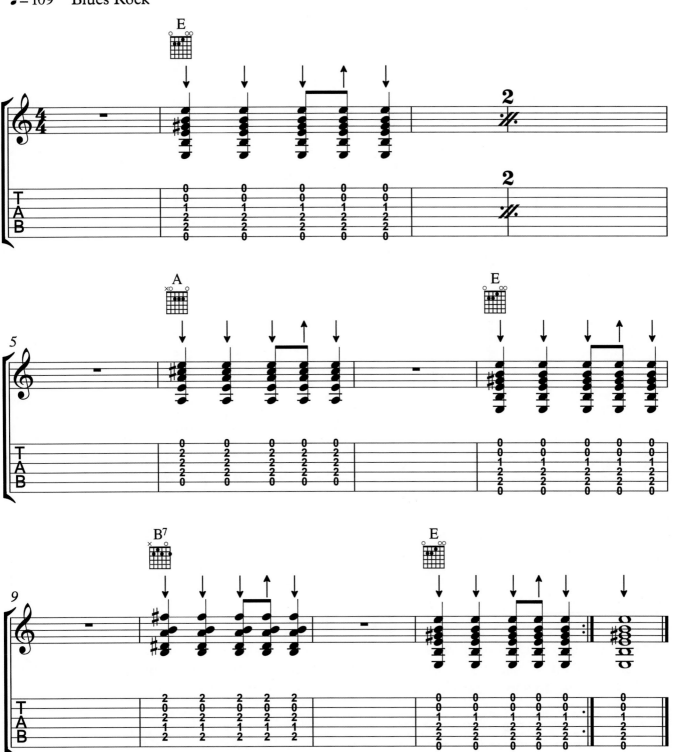

Victory At Sea

This piece uses the chords E, G, A and C. Remember to practise the chord changes before you attempt the song. Above the second bar, there is the direction *sim*. This is an abbreviation of the Italian word *simile* which means 'in a similar way' and indicates that we are to play the music in a similar manner to how the previous passage has been played. In this instance, the simile marking is referring to the strumming pattern. The strumming pattern looks like this:

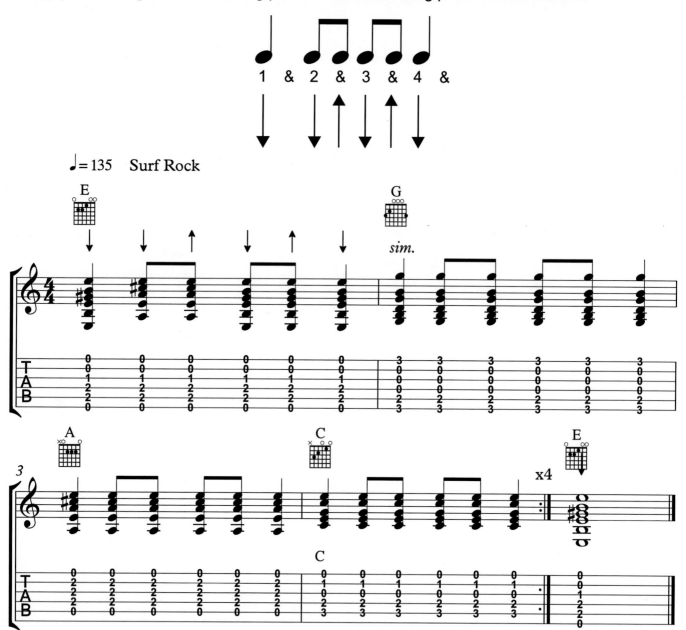

Rhythm Slashes

Sometimes when reading a piece of music that contains only chords, instead of the usual standard notation or tablature we may see **rhythm slashes**. This type of notation indicates the rhythm to be played and usually, we see the chords that are to be used written above the stave.

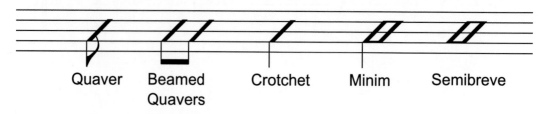

90

Candy From A Baby

Start ..../..../....

End ..../..../....

This piece mostly uses a two bar strumming pattern written out using rhythm slashes. Remember that we are using down-strums on the beat and up-strums off the beat. Watch out for the rhythm change in bars 9 and 10.

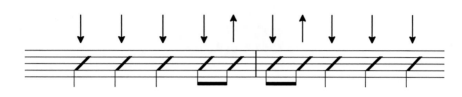

♩=126   Hard Rock

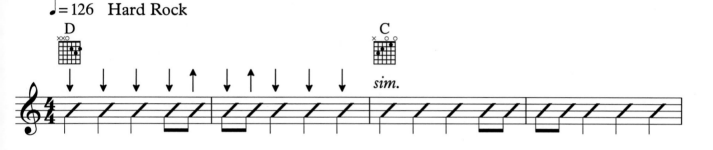

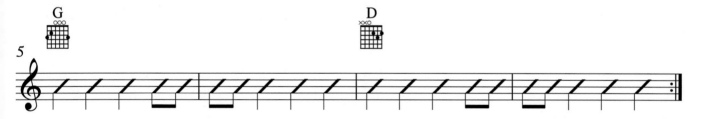

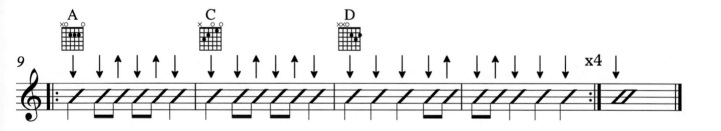

Summary

In this lesson we have learnt how to:

- Play rhythm patterns with down and up strums.
- Play the open E and B7 chords.
- Understand and play pieces with rhythm slashes.

Things To Remember

- Play down-strums on the beat and up-strums off the beat.
- Don't strum all of the strings when performing an up-strum.
- Practise the chord changes before you attempt to learn the piece.

Study Pieces

The following four pieces have been written to incorporate the skills and techniques that you have learnt throughout this book.

Tracks 182 & 183

Toothless

Start ..../..../....

End ..../..../....

93

Red Hot Chilli Pickle

♩ = 120 Funk Rock

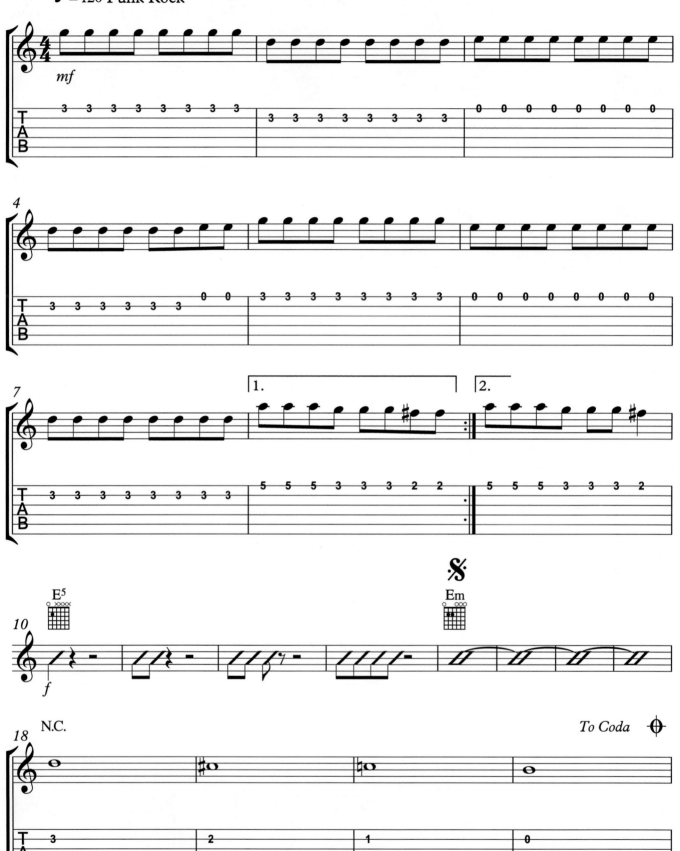

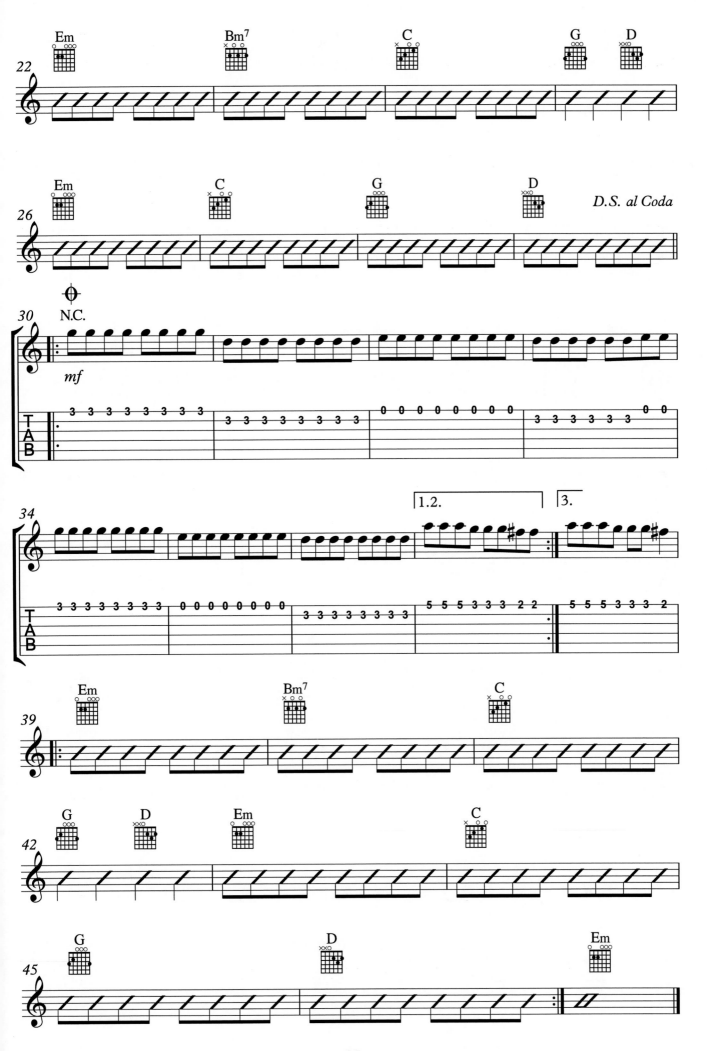

Ladybird

♩ = 140   Pop Rock

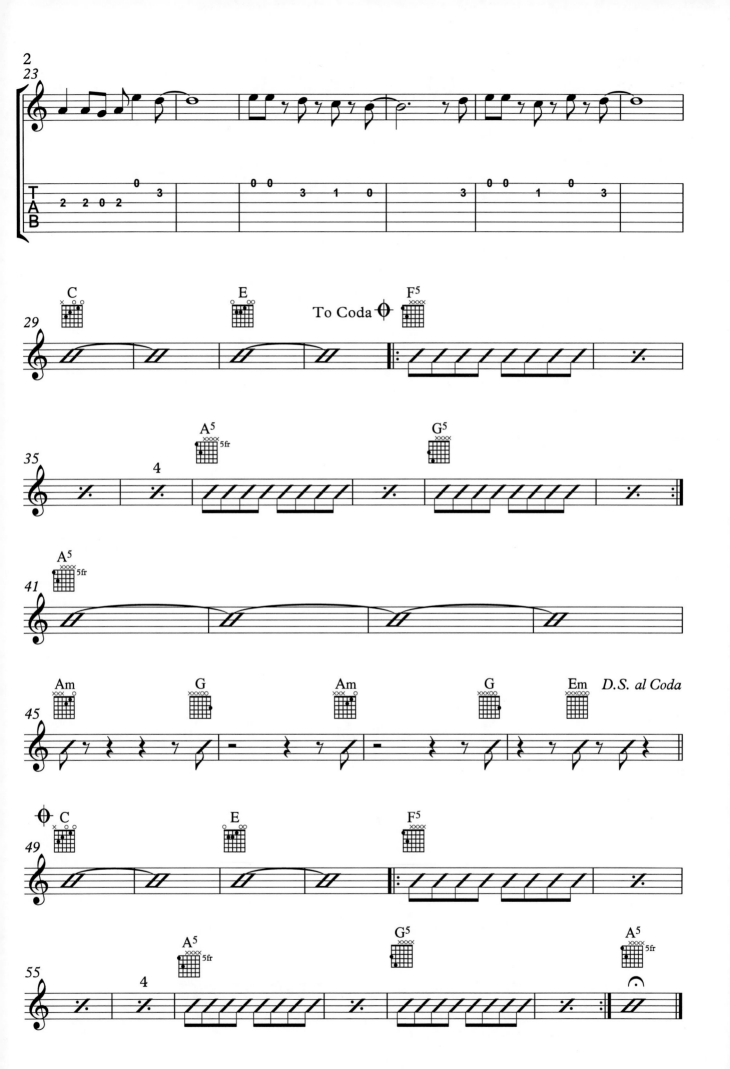

Sunnyside Blues

Appendix

Open Chords

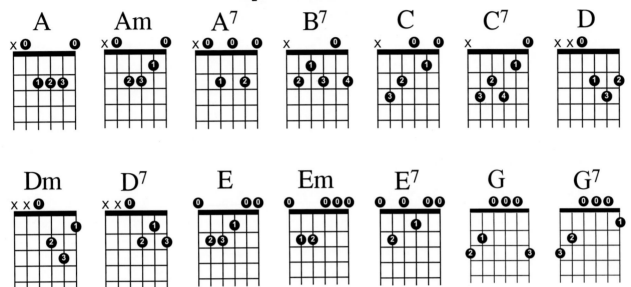

A Am A⁷ B⁷ C C⁷ D

Dm D⁷ E Em E⁷ G G⁷

Power Chords

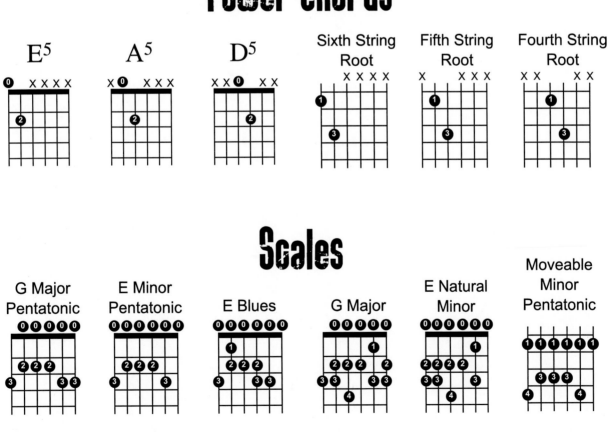

E⁵ A⁵ D⁵ Sixth String Root Fifth String Root Fourth String Root

Scales

G Major Pentatonic E Minor Pentatonic E Blues G Major E Natural Minor Moveable Minor Pentatonic